The Girls' Guide to
FRIENDS

The Girls' Guide to

FRIENDS

STRAIGHT TALK ON MAKING CLOSE PALS, CREATING LASTING TIES, AND BEING AN ALL-AROUND GREAT FRIEND

Julie Taylor

THREE RIVERS PRESS • NEW YORK

Published by Three Rivers Press, New York, New York.
Member of the Crown Publishing Group, a division of Random House, Inc.
www.randomhouse.com

THREE RIVERS PRESS and the Tugboat design are registered trademarks of Random House, Inc.

Printed in the United States of America

Design by Helene Berinsky

Library of Congress Cataloging-in-Publication Data

Taylor, Julie.
   The girls' guide to friends: straight talk on making close pals, creating lasting ties, and being an all-around great friend/Julie Taylor—1st ed.
   Summary: Explores the comforts and confusions of friendship, discussing the different kinds of friends, keeping in touch with friends, mixing romance and friendship, the impact of friendship, saving a friendship, and more.
   1. Friendship in adolescence—Juvenile literature.   2. Teenage girls—Psychology—Juvenile literature.   [1. Friendship.]   I. Title.

BF724.3.F64 .T39 2002
158.2'5'08352—dc21   2002018123

ISBN 0-609-80857-5

10 9 8 7 6 5 4 3 2 1

First Edition

For Jay and Holden Garcia Brown—
I Love You!

ACKNOWLEDGMENTS

Special thanks to Kip Kotzen, Carrie Thornton, and all of my amazing friends.

CONTENTS

YOU'VE GOTTA HAVE FRIENDS: AN INTRODUCTION   11

1. **Just Your Type**   15
   QUIZ: Who's Your Perfect Pal?

2. **Making Friends**   39
   QUIZ: Are You a Friend Magnet?

3. **How to Be a Good Friend**   55
   QUIZ: What Kind of Friend Are You?

4. **Unconventional Friends**   67
   QUIZ: How Open-Minded Are You About
   Friendship?

5. **Best Friends**   85
   QUIZ: How Well Do You Know Your Best Friend?

6. **Fight the Good Fight**   97
   QUIZ: What's Your Fighting Style?

Contents

7. **Communication Nation**   115
   QUIZ: How in Touch Are You and Your Friends?

8. **Love and Friendship**   131
   QUIZ: Do You Believe Romance and Friendship
   Can Mix?

9. **Party Time**   147
   QUIZ: What's Your Party-Girl Persona?

10. **That's What Friends Are For**   159
    QUIZ: How Good a Friend Are You When the
    Chips Are Down?

11. **Changing the World**   181
    QUIZ: What Kind of an Impact Do You and Your
    Friends Make?

12. **Friends Fallout**   195
    QUIZ: Can This Friendship Be Saved?

13. **Friends Forever**   207
    QUIZ: What's Your Friends-Forever Potential?

CONCLUSION   215

INDEX   217

YOU'VE GOTTA HAVE FRIENDS:
AN INTRODUCTION

I can't imagine my life without my friends. If they weren't around, who would cheer me up when I've had the worst day ever? Who would listen to me drone on and on about my latest boy drama and never tell me to shut up? Who would make me feel like the most important girl on the planet? Nobody, that's who. Because there are no other people in the whole world like your pals, your buds, your compadres. They're the ones who stick by you through thick and thin, the ones you can tell anything to without worrying that they'll laugh at you or think you're weird. They're the ones you obsess over *Dawson's Creek* with and talk on the phone to until the wee hours of the morning. They know your deepest, darkest secrets yet are never even a tad tempted to blab 'em all over school. They're the family you've chosen for yourselves.

But friendship, like any other relationship, can be a bit confusing. What happens when your bud blows you off for a boy? Or when your best friend hangs out with a new pal but doesn't include you? Or when you're so mad at your friend you could practically bite her head off? Good news: *The Girls' Guide to Friends* will tell you how to handle these situations and more. I'll tell you everything you've ever wanted to know about friendship by tackling issues that no magazine dares to (like how to break up with a friend or what to do if you're crushing on your boy bud) and discussing topics you might be too freaked to bring up with anyone else (such as what to do if a friend is into self-mutilation or drugs). First off, I'll show you how to figure out what type of friend your pal is—from Plastic-Fantastic to True-Blue. Then I'll teach you how to become an instant friend magnet without even trying. And, after I show you how to overcome shyness and win *anybody* over, we'll explore how you can be the coolest best friend ever! You'll also get the lowdown on cool parties you can throw with your pals and even how you and your buds can change the world. In a cyber friendship? I'll discuss how to survive one of those, too, before going over the do's and don'ts of long-distance friendship, being friends with your ex, and the joys of bonding with the 'rents. And if one of your friends turns into an enemy, you'll learn how to fight fair, know when to cut your losses and move on, and how to survive if a bud says your friendship is history. And, finally, I'll share the secrets of making your friendships last 'til your twentieth high school reunion . . . and beyond.

And, just like in my first book, *The Girls' Guide to Guys,* there's a quiz at the end of each chapter for you to take. Once you're finished, you'll know the answers to such probing questions as "Do You Believe Romance and Friendship Can Mix?" and "What's Your Friends-Forever Potential?"

The Girls' Guide to Friends is a guide just for you—written by a girl who treasures her boy buds and gal pals more than words can say. I don't claim to know it all, not by a long shot. But I know a lot about the people I call friends. They're not all still in my life, but they all continue to live in my memory. And they've taught me lessons I'll never, ever forget.

I wish I could have turned to a book like this when Tori, my best friend in junior high, talked about me behind my back and I didn't know what to do. Or a guide I could've gone to when my friend Shawn told me he was gay junior year and I wanted to say just the right thing. Or when I fell head over heels for my guy friend Steve but wasn't sure he was into me or not. Or that day my once-best friend Laura and I decided to call it quits, and I felt totally incomplete without her. I got through tough times such as these on my own, but now you don't have to. I hope the advice that fills these pages helps you and your buds have the kind of friendship that even our fave *Friends* Phoebe, Rachel, and Monica would envy: a true-blue friendship that never ends.

Love, Julie

Just Your Type

Eek—you've got a major crisis! Who do you call? Depends what your problemo is, of course. If you can't decide what to wear on your hot date, you dial up your Fashion Diva friend. Desperate to find out the skinny on tonight's big bash? Your Party Pal is the one to call. Need help cramming for that killer algebra quiz? Ring up your Study Buddy pronto! See, friends are like shoes—different ones fit different occasions. Just like you'd never be caught dead wearing your Adidas to Prom, you'd probably never count on your Party Pal to give you any major life advice. Nope, that's your Best Bud's job. Figuring out what Friend Type your pals fall under will help you determine who you can count on . . . and who you can count out. This chapter tells you all—and I do mean *all*—you need to know about the top ten friend groups. Have fun figuring which category your own friends fall into!

Party Pal

She's the one you call for the buzz on the latest bash, since she gets invited to every single party in town. You have an absolute blast every time you're with her, and when she's around you never know what's going to happen next. Here's everything you need to know about the Party Pal:

FAVORITE CLOTHES Miniskirts, sparkly shirts, and anything with fur

DEAD GIVEAWAY Those directions she's holding are to the biggest party in town

FAVORITE FOOD Party grub, of course—chips and salsa, Chex Mix, anything with a toothpick in it

FAVORITE PHRASE "Let's get this party started!"

WHAT SHE'LL BE Party planner, publicist, cruise director

NEVER MISSES TRL

TOTALLY LOOKS UP TO Kate Hudson (the party queen from *Almost Famous*)

WHERE YOU'LL GO TOGETHER Parties, clubs, happening restaurants

WHAT YOU TALK ABOUT Who's there, who's hooking up with whom, and what everybody's wearing

CALL HER WHEN You're looking for something amazing to do on a Friday night

BUT RING UP SOMEONE ELSE WHEN Your boyfriend just broke up with you and you need a shoulder to cry on

LOVES PALS WHO ARE Outgoing, fearless, and ready for anything

LOATHES PALS WHO ARE Homebodies, shy, and freaked to try new things

HANG WITH HER IF She's fun to be around, cheers you up, and always includes you in the celebratory shenanigans

DITCH HER IF She's a name-dropper, snobby, or makes you feel insecure

WORD TO THE WISE Party Pals can be totally fun to be around, but if you're in dire need of some major advice and the Party Pal blows you off for her latest bash, RSVP right out of her life.

THE LAST WORD "I have a ton of friends, but none of them are more fun than Katie is. There's never a dull moment with her around. We always manage to hit every single clambake in town. If it's happening, we're there! When I'm with her, I feel like I'm in a movie or something. She may not be my closest friend, but she's definitely the most fabulous." —Jamie, 16

Study Buddy

She's the girl with all the answers—literally. Together, you ace tests and breeze through homework, no problem! Here, the facts on the girl with *all* the facts: your Study Buddy.

FAVORITE CLOTHES Comfy clothes that are easy to think in—sweats, T-shirts, and tennis shoes

DEAD GIVEAWAY That stack of textbooks in her arms

FAVORITE FOOD Foods scientifically proven to make you smarter—fish, tofu, and peanuts

FAVORITE PHRASE "Is that your final answer?"

WHAT SHE'LL BE Scientist, professor, doctor

NEVER MISSES *Jeopardy*

TOTALLY LOOKS UP TO Claire Danes (a true Ivy League celeb)

WHERE YOU'LL GO TOGETHER The library, the symphony, the bookstore

WHAT YOU TALK ABOUT Your latest test, quiz, or homework assignment

LOVES PALS WHO ARE Focused, intelligent, and driven

LOATHES PALS WHO ARE Lazy, air-headed, or absent-minded

HANG WITH HER IF She helps you with your homework and inspires you to make better grades and reach your full potential

DITCH HER IF She always wants to copy off your assignments or constantly tries to make you feel like she's smarter than you are

WORD TO THE WISE It's a huge relief to have a Study Buddy around when you're cramming for finals or wrapping up that killer term paper. But if your Study Buddy expects you to do all the work or turns the grading system into a competition, tell her she flunked on friendship.

THE LAST WORD "I don't know how I'd make it without my friend Jenni. She studies with me at least three days a week, and we quiz each other before every major test. Since I met her, I've gone from a 2.5 grade point average to a 3.5, and my confidence level has shot through the roof. We're a mean, lean test-taking team!" —Kari, 17

Plastic Pal

Everyone has at least one friend who's a little on the plastic side. She's not 100 percent fake exactly—but when she tells you that you look amazing when you're wearing leggings and a tank, you have to wonder if she's telling you the whole truth. Get ready for the fantastic-plastic facts:

FAVORITE CLOTHES Trendy clothes that look good but don't last—little minis, halters, and clunky sandals

DEAD GIVEAWAY That fake, saccharine-sweet smile that's always plastered on her face

FAVORITE FOOD Think no calories, no flavor—fat-free cheese, baked potato chips, imitation bacon bits

FAVORITE PHRASE "You look soooooooooooo cute!"

WHAT SHE'LL BE Politician, fashion stylist, public relations exec

NEVER MISSES *Politically Incorrect*

TOTALLY LOOKS UP TO Britney Spears (who has been accused of having a few plastic parts)

WHERE YOU'LL GO TOGETHER Places everyone else goes to—amusement parks, the pool, the mall

WHAT YOU TALK ABOUT How cute you look, how cute she looks, how cute everyone else thinks you look

CALL HER WHEN You need a quick compliment and an ego boost

BUT RING UP SOMEONE ELSE WHEN You really want honest insight

LOVES PALS WHO ARE Bubbly, flattering, and eager to please

LOATHES PALS WHO ARE Brutally honest, confrontational, and controversial

HANG WITH HER IF She's fun, upbeat, and makes you feel good about yourself

DITCH HER IF She's mean-spirited, untrustworthy, or unreliable

WORD TO THE WISE Plastic Pals are superficial, but they can be tolerable as long as you don't tell them anything you don't want everyone else to know. The second she spreads rumors about you or talks bad behind your back, however, it's time to kick her to the curb.

THE LAST WORD "My friend Tina is kind of fake, but we have fun together. When I want to go dancing or have a good time, she's a great person to call. We'll never be best friends, but that's okay. Sometimes you just

want to hang out with someone you can have fun around—even if she doesn't always tell it like it is."
—Belinda, 14

Boy Bud

He's the guy you like but don't *like* like. You can tell him anything and always count on him to give you the "guy perspective." Here's all you need to know about the Boy Bud:

FAVORITE CLOTHES Jeans, Ts, baseball caps

DEAD GIVEAWAY The smile on his face after he cracks one of his infamous "guy" jokes

FAVORITE FOOD Anything and everything—buffalo wings, corn chips, Ding Dongs

FAVORITE PHRASE "What do you see in *that* guy?"

WHAT HE'LL BE Coach, stockbroker, salesman

NEVER MISSES *The Drew Carey Show*

TOTALLY LOOKS UP TO Ben Affleck (Matt Damon's boy bud)

WHERE YOU'LL GO TOGETHER The game, the arcade, the driving range

WHAT YOU TALK ABOUT Why men are from Mars and women are from Venus

LOVES PALS WHO ARE Fun, vivacious, and ready for anything

LOATHES PALS WHO ARE Bossy, super-critical, or negative

HANG WITH HIM IF He's fun, supportive, and like the big bro you never had

DITCH HIM IF He's self-centered, stuck-up, or you think he's only being friends with you in hopes you'll want something more. (Unless, that is, you start to develop feelings for him!)

WORD TO THE WISE It's great to have a guy friend you can tell anything to. And he's a perfect standby when you need a guy to go somewhere with but don't want to deal with a date. But if you think he really wants something more, show him the door.

THE LAST WORD "I've been great friends with Trevor since seventh grade. He helps me with my crushes and I help him with his. Plus, he never acts catty like some of my girlfriends do. He's always mellow and low-key, no matter what's going on around him. He's truly the best guy I know." —Mandy, 16

Old Friend

You've known this girl forever and a day. She's been there for everything—your first kiss, your first bra, even your first crush. Here's how to spot the Old Friend, a true oldie-but-goodie:

FAVORITE CLOTHES Fashion infused with history, like old concert Ts, retro low-riders, and vintage Adidases

DEAD GIVEAWAY That stack of old yearbooks she has in her room

FAVORITE FOOD Lunchbox faves—sandwiches, Rice Krispie treats, Lunchables

FAVORITE PHRASE "Do you remember the time . . . ?"

WHAT SHE'LL BE Historian, teacher, documentary film-maker

NEVER MISSES *Wonder Years* reruns

TOTALLY LOOKS UP TO Drew Barrymore (the star we've seen grow up on screen)

WHERE YOU'LL GO TOGETHER The park, the movies, your old hangouts

WHAT YOU TALK ABOUT Times you've shared, people you've known, and anything else regarding the "good old days"

CALL HER WHEN You need advice from someone who truly knows you

BUT RING UP SOMEONE ELSE WHEN You want to do something totally out of the norm

LOVES PALS WHO ARE Loyal, reliable, and dependable

LOATHES PALS WHO ARE Phony, inconsistent, and irresponsible

HANG WITH HER IF She's supportive, understanding, and would do anything for you

DITCH HER IF She's stuck in the past, judgmental, or doesn't like you to make new friends

WORD TO THE WISE Old Friends are great because they

know practically everything about you. When you say, "He's just like Chuck from three years ago," they actually know who Chuck is. You don't have to fill in the blanks. But if your Old Friend doesn't like you to make any new ones, it might be time to retire this ancient friendship.

THE LAST WORD "I've known Kelly since kindergarten. She was there when I lost my first tooth and when I broke my elbow on the playground. I love being around her because she totally gets me. When my parents got divorced, I felt like everything in my world was changing. But when I was with Kelly, I felt okay again because she is a constant source of support and always has been. She's not going anywhere."
—Tamara, 13

The Clone

She likes you so much, she wants to *be* you. She dresses like you, walks like you, and talks like you. Is this flattering or just creepy? You be the judge after reading all about The Clone:

FAVORITE CLOTHES Whatever shirts, pants, and shoes *you* wear first

DEAD GIVEAWAY The outfit she's sporting, which is identical to the one you wore yesterday

FAVORITE FOOD Whatever *you* like, 'cause your faves are her faves

FAVORITE PHRASE "Where did you get that?"

WHAT SHE'LL BE Personal assistant, magician, celebrity impersonator

NEVER MISSES *Becoming*

TOTALLY LOOKS UP TO Beyoncé from Destiny's Child (the coolest dress-alike band around)

WHERE YOU'LL GO TOGETHER Wherever you want to go, she'll follow

WHAT YOU TALK ABOUT Your likes, dislikes, and opinions on everything

CALL HER WHEN You feel like talking about yourself and want someone's total attention

BUT RING UP SOMEONE ELSE WHEN You need someone to give you a reality check

LOVES PALS WHO ARE Outgoing, dynamic, and larger-than-life

LOATHES PALS WHO ARE Timid, quiet, and inconspicuous

HANG WITH HER IF She makes you feel like you're the coolest girl in the whole, wide world

DITCH HER IF She kisses your butt so bigtime, even *you* get sick of the royal treatment

WORD TO THE WISE The Clone thinks you rule, so she's totally flattering to be around. But if she brown-noses you so much that even you're annoyed by the mere sight of her, it's time to ditch this groupie.

THE LAST WORD "My friend Angie totally looks up to me. She had her hair cut like me and she dresses the exact same way I do. It's neat to have someone think I'm so cool. I like influencing her fashion sense, and she's a real boost to my ego." —Hannah, 14

Gossip Queen

She knows everything about everything and is dying to dish the latest dirt. She's so in the know, she finds out about breakups five minutes before they even happen. Get ready for all you need to know about the Gossip Queen:

FAVORITE CLOTHES Form-fitting fashions that attract attention—tiny tops paired with tight capris

DEAD GIVEAWAY That devilish smile she gets before she spills the scoop

FAVORITE FOOD Food that everybody is talking about but no one can pronounce—like bruschetta, couscous, or chai tea

FAVORITE PHRASE "You'll *never* believe this!"

WHAT SHE'LL BE Gossip columnist, spokesperson, novelist

NEVER MISSES *The E! True Hollywood Story*

TOTALLY LOOKS UP TO Melissa Rivers (because her gossipy rants on the red carpet crack her up)

WHERE YOU'LL GO TOGETHER House parties, clubs, happening restaurants

WHAT YOU TALK ABOUT Who's dating who and who's dumping who

CALL HER WHEN You're dying to hear the latest

BUT RING UP SOMEONE ELSE WHEN You need to confide a major secret

LOVES PALS WHO ARE Outgoing, outspoken, and outlandish

LOATHES PALS WHO ARE Introverted, guarded, and dignified

HANG WITH HER IF You love how you never know what she'll say next

DITCH HER IF She's malicious or likes to make your secrets front-page news

WORD TO THE WISE Gossip Queens love to talk the talk, and they're a trip to be around. But if you're the subject of their latest gossip session, dump 'em and *really* give 'em something to talk about.

THE LAST WORD "If you want to know something, ask Lori. She knows everything about what's going on— and I do mean everything. I can listen to the girl talk for hours! She is so hilarious and witty. I wouldn't want her gossiping about me, but I love hearing her gossip about everybody else. She knows it all."
—Kim, 17

Cyber Pal

You've never met her face to face, but you're super close. When something major happens, she's always just a click away. Here's everything you need to know about the Cyber Pal:

FAVORITE CLOTHES Anything shiny, silver, or orange

DEAD GIVEAWAY Those chipped fingernails, an unfortunate result of too many hours at the keyboard

FAVORITE FOOD Anything she can eat at her computer desk—popcorn, sodas, chips

FAVORITE PHRASE "You've got mail!"

WHAT SHE'LL BE Computer programmer, Web site designer, online entrepreneur

NEVER MISSES *Alias*

TOTALLY LOOKS UP TO Bill Gates (the king of the computer world!)

WHERE YOU'LL GO TOGETHER Chat rooms, Web sites, and cyberspace

WHAT YOU TALK ABOUT E-mail, downloads, DSL, and life in general

CALL HER WHEN E-mail just isn't going to cut it

BUT RING UP SOMEONE ELSE WHEN You want to hang out face-to-face

LOVES PALS WHO ARE Articulate, interactive, and computer-savvy

LOATHES PALS WHO ARE Incomprehensible, vague, and untruthful

HANG WITH HER IF Her e-mails totally make your day

DITCH HER IF You suspect she's not really who she says she is

WORD TO THE WISE Cyber Pals are great companions down life's superhighway. But if you suspect your seventeen-year-old female Cyber Pal is really some forty-three-year-old male pervert, sign off from this friendship immediately.

THE LAST WORD "I haven't met Geneva in person, but she's one of my closest friends. I feel like she knows the real me. We e-mail and instant-message each other at least five times a day. Even though she lives across the country, she's always close to my heart." —Sara, 14

Fashion Diva

She's so put together, she always looks like she just walked off a runway. When you feel the urge to splurge, she's the perfect shopping partner. Read on for more fashion facts about the Fashion Diva:

FAVORITE CLOTHES Anything that's cutting-edge and in style—leopard pants, designer tops, way-too-expensive shoes

DEAD GIVEAWAY Daddy's American Express gold card in her perfectly manicured hand

FAVORITE FOOD Food that looks as good as it tastes—sushi, truffles, and tarts

FAVORITE PHRASE "Go ahead—try it on!"

WHAT SHE'LL BE Fashion designer, architect, interior decorator

NEVER MISSES *House of Style*

TOTALLY LOOKS UP TO Carrie Bradshaw of *Sex and the City* (fashion consumer extraordinaire)

WHERE YOU'LL GO TOGETHER The mall, specialty shops, and anywhere you can show off your latest look

WHAT YOU TALK ABOUT Cool designers, fashion faux pas, and the latest *Vogue*

CALL HER WHEN You need the perfect outfit pronto!

BUT RING UP SOMEONE ELSE WHEN You feel like renting movies and chilling in your grubbiest gear

LOVES PALS WHO ARE Stylish, hip, and fashion-forward

LOATHES PALS WHO ARE Frumpy, disheveled, and behind the times

HANG WITH HER IF She inspires you to tap into your Inner Supermodel

DITCH HER IF She puts down your sense of style

WORD TO THE WISE Fashion Diva friends are the ones to call when you're having a real-life fashion emergency. But if they continually try to make you feel like they're way cooler than you are, put this friendship back in the closet.

THE LAST WORD "I have a blast shopping with Stella. She picks outfits I'd never even consider buying and makes them looks like a million bucks. We always have an amazing time together." —Traci, 16

Best Bud

When anything happens to you—big or small—she's the first one you call. You can tell her anything and everything, and she's the one person who never lets you down. Read on for the 4-1-1 on your Best Bud:

FAVORITE CLOTHES Anything that's yours, since you love trading clothes

DEAD GIVEAWAY The note in her back pocket—from you, of course!

FAVORITE FOOD Chocolate-chip cookie dough that you make together from scratch

FAVORITE PHRASE "Anything you need, I'll be there."

WHAT SHE'LL BE Therapist, nurse, social worker

NEVER MISSES *Friends*

TOTALLY LOOKS UP TO Jennifer Love Hewitt (the friendliest star around)

WHERE YOU'LL GO TOGETHER Your house, her house, the mall

WHAT YOU TALK ABOUT Who you like, who she likes, and practically everything else you can think of

CALL HER WHEN You really need someone to talk to

BUT RING UP SOMEONE ELSE WHEN You want a second opinion on something

LOVES PALS WHO ARE Sweet, loyal, and understanding

LOATHES PALS WHO ARE Two-faced, fake, and rude

HANG WITH HER IF She supports you completely, would never betray your trust, and always manages to make you feel a zillion times better

DITCH HER IF She's too possessive, jealous, or blabs your deepest secrets around school

WORD TO THE WISE Best Buds got their name for a reason—they're the best. But if your best friend wants to be your *only* friend, she might be due for a demotion.

THE LAST WORD "My best friend and I do everything together. She's like the sister I never had. She knows exactly what I'm going to say before I even say it. We're so on the same wavelength, it's almost scary! When we're together, I feel like I can conquer the world. I would do absolutely anything for that girl."
—Joni, 14

QUIZ
Who's Your Perfect Pal?

1. What's your ideal way to spend a Saturday with friends?

   a) Going to the movies
   b) Hanging at the park
   c) Hitting a hot new restaurant
   d) Shopping, then clubbing
   e) Chilling on the homefront

2. What do you most like to talk about with pals?

   a) Old times
   b) What's going on at school
   c) People you know
   d) Fashion and beauty
   e) Your thoughts and feelings

3. What's your favorite thing to do in your spare time?

   a) Have heart-to-hearts with your friends
   b) Read, watch TV, and hang
   c) Go places to see and be seen
   d) Dance up a storm
   e) Scribble in your journal

4. What's the most important part of friendship?

   a) Sharing a deep, emotional bond
   b) Having someone to hang with
   c) Having someone to talk to

d) Having fun

e) Being supported and encouraged

5. It's the last day of school. What do you do to celebrate?

a) Invite a few friends to sleep over

b) Go to a sporting event

c) Invite everyone you know to a party at your house

d) Meet your friends at an all-ages dance club

e) Hang at home

6. What's your favorite animal?

a) Dog

b) Cat

c) Parakeet

d) Leopard

e) Owl

7. What's the sweetest thing a friend could do for you right after a breakup?

a) Listen to you

b) Tell you that your ex is a jerk

c) Rehash the breakup details over and over again

d) Drag you out on the town

e) Tell you that you rule

8. What's your favorite thing to wear with a T-shirt?

　　a)　Your favorite PJ bottoms
　　b)　A pair of jeans
　　c)　Your cutest miniskirt
　　d)　A tight pair of leather pants
　　e)　Your comfiest sweats

Who's your perfect pal? To find out, check to see if you have more As, Bs, Cs, Ds, or Es.

Mostly As: True-Blue Bud
You're drawn to friends who are honest, dependable, and caring. Yep—you love being able to tell your pals anything and knowing that your secrets are safe with them. Cool! You'd much rather hang with your best friends on a Saturday night than hit some crowded party. Who wants to be with a rowdy group of strangers when you could chill with your closest chums instead? Not you! You're more into connecting than carousing. Going out to eat, catching a flick, and having sleepovers are your friend functions of choice. And since you love to bond with your babes, don't worry—the True-Blue Bud will open up to you completely, making it easy to forge a fast, long-lasting friendship.
Friend Connections: Best Bud, Old Friend

Mostly Bs: Hang-Out Homey

Friends who like to hang out and chill are right up your alley. You love the fact you can totally be yourself around them, and when they're around you never have to dress to impress. You have a blast hanging at the arcade, park, or bowling alley, but you also have fun doing nothing at all. Just being around these pals is more than enough. This is a simple kind of friendship—no dramas, traumas, or catfights. And that's just how you like it, thankyouverymuch.
Friend Connections: Boy Bud, The Clone

Mostly Cs: Chatty Chum

You're into friends who can talk the talk as well as you can. The art of conversation is your specialty, so you need girlfriends who were also born with the gift of gab. You're a sucker for a juicy bit of gossip, and you absolutely live for marathon phone conversations that go on forever and ever. When it comes to hitting the town, forget going to the movies or seeing a play—you're more into activities where you can work your vocal chords. Having deep, dish-filled discussions at a cool restaurant or party (preferably packed with people you can talk about) is more your speed. As long as you and your pals believe chatter matters, your friendships will continue to be the talk of the town.
Friend Connections: Plastic Pal, Gossip Queen

Mostly Ds: Adventurous Amigo

You like friends who work as hard and play as hard as you do. You need extreme action 24/7—and these pleasure-seeking pals provide it. Whether you're shopping up a storm or bungee-jumping off a cliff, you all live life to the fullest. No boring weekends for you! Nope—you like to spend your free time preening and partying at the most happening hotspots. With the Adventurous Amigo by your side, you can do anything—and look damn good doing it, too.

Friend Connections: Party Pal, Fashion Diva

Mostly Es: Brainy Babe

No airheaded amigos for you, please. You like friends you can truly connect with on an emotional and intellectual level. Don't get me wrong—you like to have as much fun as the next girlie. But you'd rather do something that challenges you—like see a foreign flick or go to the symphony—than chow down with the local yokels at the pizza joint. You need art, culture, excitement—and these friends will help you find it. They don't think going to a museum is boring, and they don't think van Gogh is an offshoot of Van Halen. Plus, you can have real conversations with them about real issues that actually matter. Who'da thunk it?!

Friend Connections: Cyber Pal, Study Buddy

2

Making Friends

In your preschool days, making friends was simple. You walked up to a kid who looked nice, said "Wanna play?" and you were best buds for life. Now that you're a little older and *a lot* wiser, making friends is a bit more tricky. How do you approach someone without looking needy? What if she already has enough friends and doesn't want any more? Or what if he doesn't like you and thinks you're a geek? Insecurities such as these often flood your mind before you're even out of the gate, stopping you dead in your tracks. But not anymore! This chapter is guaranteed to give you that shove in the right direction you so desperately need. Because making friends is way easier than you think—especially when you master these tricks of the trade.

Friends Forever

How do you make a friend for life? The easiest way is to be one. Okay, we've all heard that before . . . but what does being a good friend mean exactly? Well, friendship is essentially about being there for the other person. When she needs to vent, listen. When he needs advice, pull a Dear Abby and lay your words of wisdom on him pronto. Of course, friendship is also about having fun together and obsessing about your latest crushes together. But that can only happen when you really trust each other, and the key to earning someone's trust is to be reliable and dependable. Don't blow them off. When you say you're going to do something for them, do it. Follow through. Sometimes it's easier said than done, but it's what friendship is all about. So, before we go any further, repeat after me: *"I will always be there for my friends one hundred percent, and they'll always be there for me!"* Words to live by.

Meet and Greet

Now that you know what makes up a good friendship, where do you meet potential friends? School is the most obvious choice, since that's where you spend most of your time. And your classes are a great place to start. When you bond with someone in Bio, you instantly have tons to talk about: the latest lab assignment, the teacher's funky haircut, the cute guy who sits in the front row. Clubs are another great place to meet people, because if you're in the same club, then odds are that you have similar interests. Ditto for sports teams. There's always major bonding over basketball, soccer, and the like.

After school, a great place to make pals is at school-sponsored events, like sporting events and dances. They sometimes sound pretty lame, but don't count them out until you give them at least one shot. After-school jobs are also a possibility. I met some of my best friends when I worked at a theme restaurant on weekends to make some extra dough, and I never would have met them if it hadn't been for that job. And hanging anywhere other teens go—the movies, the mall, wherever—is another good way to meet fun people. As my mom used to say, "You can't meet anybody while you're sitting in your room!" Truer words have never been spoken. So get out there and mingle! Don't deprive the rest of the world of knowing a cool girl like you.

Chum Criteria

Okay, you've taken my advice and are out there scoping for new buds. Now what? First, you've got to know what you're looking for in a friend. While it's true that no two friends are exactly alike, there are certain universal qualities that most cool friends share. Here are the top five:

1. Honesty: When a friend says something to you, you want to be able to believe it. Obviously, you can't tell the first time you meet someone if she's a liar (unless she tells you she's a weekend VJ for MTV). But if you catch someone in a lot of little white lies, that's a major red flag. Is this really someone you want to be friends with? In friendship, that old cliché is true: Honesty is the best policy.

2. Common Interests: When you have things in common, you'll have more to talk about. It can be *anything:* You both love Blink-182; you play tennis; you're totally into *Angel.* Yes, sometimes opposites attract—but when you have at least a few things in common, the friendship just seems to click.

3. Reliability: You want to be able to count on your pals. Does she call when she says she will? When she makes plans with you on Friday night, does she always keep them? It's tiny things like this that let you know you can count on her in a major way.

4. Trustworthiness: Without trust, you've got nothing. But trust has got to be earned. When you tell her a secret, does she keep it to herself instead of blabbing it all over school? When you ask her a question, does she give you an honest answer rather than just telling you what you want to hear? This is what trust is all about.

5. Thoughtfulness: When it comes to friendship, little things mean a lot. Does she remember things like your birthday and you and your b-friend's anniversary? When you have a big test coming up, does she offer to help you study? You want to know that your pals are thinking of you as much as you're thinking about them.

Pal Pickup Lines

When you meet someone you think would be cool to be friends with, it's sometimes hard to know the right thing to say. You don't want to sound geeky, lame, or desperate. But never fear. Just lay one of the following lines on a potential pal, and your friendship is guaranteed to sizzle instead of fizzle.

- IN CLASS: Did you study for the big test?
  Think of something that's going on in the class (a big paper, quiz, or project) and ask her about it. Since you're both going through the same experience, she'll totally feel your pain.

- OUTSIDE OF SCHOOL: Aren't you in my algebra class?
  When you're outside of school, spotting someone who walks the same hallowed halls can instantly bond you. Approach and make your move!

- AT THE MALL: That skirt looks fab on you!
  Who can resist a compliment? Telling her you like her style (and meaning it) is an instant ice-breaker.

- IN THE CAF: Not salisbury steak *again*!
No one likes cafeteria food—so she'll happily join in when you bemoan the day's culinary offerings. *Bon appétit!*

- AT A PARTY: Chips and dip?
Offering to help the hostess with the mostest serve snacks gives you an excuse to talk to every person in the room. And who can resist a chick with Cheetos?

- AT A MEETING: What can I do to help?
When you're in a club, there are always a million things to do but never enough people to do them. Offer to help circulate petitions, make posters, or organize food drives, and suddenly you're the most popular girl in the room.

- AT A CLUB: Doesn't this place *rule*?
When you're both into something, you'll experience a kind of Mutual-Admiration-Society bonding when you realize that you like the same things. Works like a charm.

- AT A MOVIE: Thumbs up or thumbs down?
After you see her coming out of the same movie you just saw, it's the perfect opp to ask her for her official Ebert-and-Roeper–style movie review. This is bound to lead into a conversation about the stupid storyline, Brad Pitt's abs, or any other pertinent information. Two thumbs up!

NEW KID ON THE BLOCK

When it comes to potential new pals, there is perhaps none more ripe for the picking than the new kid in school. After all, this person knows *no one* and is just dying to meet someone who'll show her the ropes. For some reason, most people tend to avoid the new kid, making her feel all the more uncomfortable. But this just paves the way for you to dive in and save the day. Go up to her and introduce yourself. Ask her where she's from and how she likes the school so far. Invite her to have lunch with you and your pals in the caf. Think of yourself as the school's unofficial Welcome Wagon, an ambassador of goodwill to every new person who walks through the doors. This is a great way to meet new people, and you'll be doing a good deed to boot.

Mixing It Up

When you make new pals, it's almost inevitable that you'll want to introduce them to your old-school buds. But sometimes new friends and old friends just don't mix at first. Why? Your old pals might feel jealous or threatened, thinking that because you've got new friends you are going to forget your old ones. In other words, they feel replaced. And your new buds might feel freaked or alienated around your old ones, simply because you share such a long history that they're not a part of.

But this doesn't mean that they can't all be one big happy family—not by a long shot. You just have to introduce them in a way that makes everyone feel comfortable. Throwing a party is an ideal way for your two worlds to collide. Play games that encourage your guests to interact and mingle. (Check out "Mind Games" on page 151 for some suggestions.) That way, your pals can get to know each other without experiencing that "What-do-I-say-*now*?" awkwardness.

If you don't go the party route, you can always just invite your new friend along the next time you hang out with your old friends. Make sure she feels included by asking her lots of questions and filling her in on any private jokes you and your pals crack along the way. But don't pay so much attention to her that you end up ignoring your other friends. When you keep things even-Steven, everybody wins!

When you make new friends, don't tell them things you DON'T like about your old friends, or vice versa. When you tell your new pal Kiley you can't stand how your old friend Laura always talks about her boyfriend and then you tell Laura how Kiley's N'Sync obsession drives you nuts, it will be hard for Kiley and Laura to be friends at all. Everyone is going to irk you sometimes (just like you'll irk people, too), but resist the urge to confide in one pal about the other one. It might make you feel better in the short term, but it will only lead to trouble in the end.

What's a Girl to Do?

Now you've made lots of new friends, and your new pals are getting along smashingly with your old ones. You want to have *fun* . . . and you want to have it now! If you're sick of doing the same old thing—movies, pizza, yawn!—it's time to shake things up a bit. Here, ten fab things to do with your friends:

1. Throw an old-fashioned slumber party.

Invite your favorite friends over for some pillow talk and experience a true blast from the past. Give each other makeovers, order in Chinese food, and prank call cute guys with the classic "Is your refrigerator running?/You better go catch it" gag. Don't forget to freeze each other's bras for old times' sake.

2. Go on a picnic with your pals.

Instead of heading to Mickey D's for lunch, why not dine al fresco in a beautiful locale? Pack your basket with unmessy finger food like sandwiches, chips, and fruit; bottles of water; a fuzzy blanket to sit on; and a frisbee to toss around after you've chowed. Lunch has never been this fun!

3. Host a "junk night."

Invite your friends over and indulge every guilty pleasure you've got! Pig out on junk foods like microwave burritos and nachos and rent the cheesiest movies you can find. Devour all the tabloids, giving each other quizzes on hot news like Michael Jackson's latest plastic-surgery procedure. You'll feel ill in the morning but strangely satisfied, too.

4. Trade clothes with your chums.

You know that skirt you absolutely can't stand anymore and that shirt that is simply the wrong color for you? Drag 'em out of the closet, call your friends, and tell them to bring over their castoffs pronto. Then you can have an all-out trade-off. When you're done, you'll all feel like you have a new wardrobe . . . without spending a cent!

5. Have a monthly Girls' Night Out.

Declare the first Friday of the month Girls' Night. No dates, no boys, no excuses! This gives you the perfect chance to bond with the babes, gossip about hotties, and catch that chick flick that your boyfriend refuses to see with you. Girl power!

6. Take a road trip (even if it's to the next town).

Does your hometown seem like a total bore? Maybe it's time for a change of scenery! Ask your mom or aunt to drive you to the next town, then explore it like you're a tourist on vacation. You'll have a blast hanging with new people and checking out the sights. Don't forget to bring a camera!

7. Make a huge deal out of your friends' birthdays.

If it happens to be one of your buds' b-day, go all out! Bake a cake with her name on it. Throw her a surprise party with all of your pals. Buy her tons of little trinkets and individually wrap each one. Sing her "Happy Birthday" right in the middle of the caf. Bring a tiara to school and make her wear it all day. She'll feel like she's the luckiest girl in the world to have a friend who's as sweet as you.

8. Make your own "Road Rules."

Hooked on MTV's *Road Rules*? You don't have to be one of their chosen few to live a life of adventure. Round up your best buds and brainstorm twenty things you've always wanted to try—like scuba diving, fly-fishing, or snowboarding. Then, vow to do one activity per week for twenty weeks. At the end of your journey, treat yourself with a handsome reward—an aromatherapy massage at a posh spa or dinner at the yummiest restaurant in town.

9. Throw a makeover party.

When you and your pals feel like you're stuck in a rut, yank yourselves out by experimenting with your looks.

Dye your pal's friend bright red or let her Mehndi the top of your feet. Not ready to go over the top? Something as simple as a new nail polish or lipstick can recharge your look effortlessly. Then have a blast showing off the "new you" at a party or all-ages club later that night. Party time!

10. Play "No Way!"

The next time you and your pals can't think of anything to do, break out your local paper and check out the entertainment listings. Everyone has to cut out one thing they would never want to do in a million years—like go to a polka dance, Bingo session, or monster-truck rally. Choose any activity that makes you say, "No way!" Then put all of the undesirable activities into a hat and choose one. That's what you're doing tonight! It'll be a trip to share a new, off-the-wall experience. And sometimes the things you least want to do end up being the most fun. This is the stuff that lifelong memories are made of!

QUIZ
Are You a Friend Magnet?

1. You notice a new person standing alone in the cafeteria on the first day of school. You

   a) immediately introduce yourself and ask her to join you.

b) smile at her briefly, then continue talking to your friends.

c) keep eating. She's not *your* problem!

2. You're hanging by the chips-and-dip table at a friend's party when a girl you've never met before comes over to dip her chip. When she says hi, you say

a) "Hi!" then ask her if she's having fun at the party.

b) "Hey!" then walk away.

c) Nothing. You don't know her, after all.

3. When you're hanging at the mall, you see a girl wearing the exact same miniskirt as you. You

a) walk up and tell her she has *terrific* taste.

b) give her a thumbs up as you pass by.

c) hightail it the other way so she won't notice your twin styles.

4. You're working at a drive-thru window when a cool chick with fuzzy dice hanging from her rearview mirror drives through. You

a) say "Cool dice!" then ask her where she got them.

b) flash her a friendly smile as you hand over her food.

c) think she looks cool but say nothing besides, "Ketchup with that?"

5. You're hanging in the back of the classroom, minding your own business. A girl you've seen before but never talked to sits next to you. You

a) ask her if she finished the homework from last night.

b) smile but say nothing.

c) get up and move.

6. You're sitting on the school bus, and there's an empty seat beside you. A guy from your English class gets on, obviously looking for a place to park. You

a) wave him over and ask if he wants to sit by you.

b) scoot over by the window in case he wants to sit down.

c) put your books in the vacant seat so he can't sit by you.

7. You and your pals are shaking your groove thang at a rockin' dance club. You notice a really hip girl dancing solo right behind you. You

a) widen your circle so she can boogie by you and your pals.

b) move a few inches closer to her, figuring if she wants to dance by you guys, *she* can make a move.

c) ignore her. You're dancing with your friends, so who cares about anybody else?

8. You're laying out in your front yard when you notice a U-haul pull up next door. You

   a) go over and introduce yourself to the new neighbors.

   b) shoot them a wave when they glance your way.

   c) roll over and hope they don't talk to you.

Do you have more As, Bs, or Cs? Tally them up to measure your friend magnetism.

Mostly As: Major Magnet
Whoa—are you friendly or what? Everywhere you go, you attract friends like bees to honey. Your sweet smile, outgoing personality, and upbeat attitude are simply irresistible to everyone you meet. As long as you don't let people take advantage of your giving nature, your life will be friend-filled and action-packed.

Mostly Bs: On-and-Off Attracter
You're always polite but would never go up and talk to someone you don't know. Instead of being overtly friendly, you prefer to send subtle signals and wait for potential friends to come to you. That's cool and all, but you could be losing possible pals if your cues go unnoticed. If you make a move now and then, your friend count will shoot through the roof.

Mostly Cs: Push-Away Pal

You sure as heck don't go out of your way to be nice to new people. In fact, some could accuse you of pushing them away. Maybe you're too shy to approach someone you don't know. Or perhaps you feel you have enough friends already and just aren't interested in making any more. Whatever your reasons, it's time to trade in the Ice Queen act for a friendlier demeanor. Once you do, your social life will soar.

3

How to Be a Good Friend

I have a handful of best friends I wouldn't trade for the world. They've been there for me through everything—major life decisions, humongous crushes, bitter breakups, and even the death of my amazing mom. Every day I try to be as good to them as they've been to me. But since there's no Friendship 101 class offered in any school that I know of, it's sometimes hard to know exactly *how* to be a good friend. Luckily for you, this chapter will fill you in on how to be the best friend you can be. Listen up!

Be All You Can Be

If you want to be the kind of friend everyone considers a "keeper," you've got to start by valuing your friendships. Think about how you'd feel about a pair of one-carat diamond earrings you got for your birthday. You'd feel so lucky to have them. You'd look at them and marvel over how awesome they are. And you'd want to do anything you could to protect them from harm. And this is how you should feel about your pals. After all, they're more precious than diamonds or gold—and they should be treated as such.

THE TEN COMMANDMENTS OF
GOOD FRIENDSHIP

1. Thou shall never intentionally hurt her feelings.
2. Thou shall listen attentively to her story about her latest crush, even if you have heard it a million times before.
3. Thou shall never go after her boyfriend, as he's off limits.
4. Thou shall never blow her off for a guy, no matter how badly you want to.
5. Thou shall offer her the best advice you possibly can whenever she needs it.
6. Thou shall console her after a bad haircut, convincing her it looks way better than it does.
7. Thou shall help her study for that big test, even when you'd rather be watching *Buffy*.
8. Thou shall let her know how important she is in your life, because she needs to hear it now and then.

9. Thou shall never badmouth her to someone else, no matter how much she's getting on your nerves.

10. Thou shall tell her your deepest, darkest thoughts, because that's what true friends are for.

The thing to always keep in mind when dealing with your compadres is that you should treat them the way you'd like them to treat you. Say your best bud is named Beth. If you wouldn't like Beth to badmouth you to your mutual friend Suzie, then don't badmouth Beth to Suzie, either. If you'd like Beth to remember your birthday without your having to remind her a zillion times, then you've got to do the same for her. In friendship, you often get as much (or as little) as you give.

Now, nobody's perfect—including you. So there are going to be times that you let your friends down, just like there will be times they let you down. But a big part of friendship is forgiveness. True friends will forgive and forget your shortcomings. And you'll do the same for them.

Listen Up

Perhaps the biggest component of being a good friend is knowing how to listen. You might be thinking, "Duh! I have ears, so obviously I know how to listen." But it's not that simple. Listening is an art form, and once you master it, your friendships will be much stronger and built to go the distance.

Think about what goes on in your head when a friend is telling you a long, involved story. Does your mind tend to wander a bit about all that homework you've got to do later on, that cute new guy in English, or what you're having for dinner? Do you start strategizing what you're going to say next instead of tuning in to what she's saying? Don't feel bad—*everybody's* done this at one time or another. I know I certainly have! I recently noticed I was always missing cues in a conversation or interrupting my pals' thoughts—so much so that I was even starting to annoy myself! That's when I decided to really concentrate during every conversation I had with my pals. This is what experts call "active listening." I couldn't believe the difference it made! When you truly listen to your friends, you'll be amazed at how much you learn from them—and how much you've been missing by tuning them out. Plus, they'll feel so much more valued when you ask them about little things they've said to you along the way. Say your pal casually mentions that she's got a killer quiz coming up in algebra. When you ask her how the quiz went a few days later, she'll feel like what she's been saying really matters.

Want to be a better listener? Start by simply deciding

to be one. Before you have a conversation with someone, tell yourself you're truly going to focus on what she's saying. Concentrate. Then look her straight in the eyes. When you make eye contact with someone (instead of looking around at everybody else in the room), she'll feel like you're interested in her and only her. And be sure to watch your body language. Don't fold your arms or turn away from who is talking, because that can put barriers between you. Stay focused.

Never take control of the conversation. If a friend is talking about the No Doubt concert she went to, it will be tempting to chime in and tell her that you love No Doubt, too. But wait until she has made her point before you make yours.

If you use these listening techniques, your friends will respect you more because they'll feel like you respect them more. And once you start *listening* to your friends instead of just *hearing* them, you'll learn tons more from each and every conversation.

Just Do It

How can you show your friends how much you care? Actions speak louder than words. Doing little things for your pals lets them know you're thinking of them and that they're important to you. Here, twenty things you can do for your friends:

FRIENDLY GESTURES

1. Write her a note listing all of the amazing times you've had together.

2. Send her a postcard saying that your life wouldn't be the same without her in it.

3. Bake her cookies and leave them in her locker with a note that says, "You're a real sweetie!"

4. Make a scrapbook for her filled with pictures, ticket stubs, notes, and memorabilia of all your times together.

5. Create an audio friendship letter telling her how much she means to you and leave it in the tape player of her car.

6. When she breaks up with someone, make her a Breakup Care Package, complete with Kleenex, her favorite magazines, and tons of junk food.

7. Leave her a daisy under the windshield wiper of her car.

8. Let her wear that shirt of yours she's in love with . . . even if you were planning on wearing it yourself!

9. Be her "secret pal" by leaving anonymous trinkets in her locker. You'll make her day, her week, even her year!

10. When her fave band comes to town, camp out for primo tickets.

11. Play her favorite song on her answering machine.

12. E-mail her little-known facts about her favorite celebs.

13. Start a Web site in her honor.

14. Treat her to an entire day of beauty by giving her a manicure, pedicure, and facial.

15. Send her flowers on August 1, International Friendship Day.

16. Treat her to a "You Pick It" Night—she gets to pick the movie, the restaurant, the topic of conversation. Whatever she says goes!

17. Place a classified ad in the local newspaper telling the world how much she rules.

18. Dedicate a song to her on her favorite radio station.

19. Offer to do her makeup and hair before a big night out.

20. Make her a mix tape of all the songs that remind you of your times together.

THE IMPORTANCE OF FRIENDSHIP

Why is it so important to do little things for your friends to let them know how much you care? Because your friends are the family you choose for yourselves. They are the ones who will be there for you through thick and thin, the ones you can tell *anything* to. And if they don't feel important and valued in your life, your friendship can easily suffer or even dissolve as a result. A lot of times we focus so much on romantic relationships and crushes that we totally neglect the other relationships in our lives. But friendship is just as important as romantic love . . . if not more so. Because odds are your friends will be around way longer than your boyfriends will. And they're the ones you'll turn to when the romance fizzles instead of sizzles. *Nobody* can make you feel better than your friends can, bottom line. Friends rule!

QUIZ
What Kind of Friend Are You?

1. Your best bud just got dumped by her longtime love. What do you do to cheer her up?

   a) Have a long heart-to-heart with her. She needs to talk it out.

   b) Drag her to the movies. You've got to get her mind off him.

   c) Buy her some flowers to boost her sagging spirits.

2. Your friend Jodi wants to hang out this Friday night. What do you suggest you do?

   a) Have a sleepover where you can bond all night.

b) Hit that new dance club that everyone's talking about.

c) Shop till you drop at the mall.

3. Your parents are at each other's throats lately, and you are about to go ballistic. What do you do?

a) Call up your friend and vent for over an hour.

b) Go bowling with your pals to work out your frustrations.

c) Tell your buds to meet you at the mall for an impromptu shopping spree.

4. Sara, your best friend, feels really lousy about herself these days. What do you do to boost her spirits?

a) Ask her what's going on, and really listen.

b) Take her rollerblading to get her mind off her troubles.

c) Treat her to a meal at her favorite restaurant.

5. It's your friend's birthday, and you want to go all out. What do you do?

a) Invite a few friends over to your house for a small, cozy gathering.

b) Throw her a slammin' party at the miniature golf course.

c) Buy her that jacket she's been drooling over for months.

6. Uh-oh! Your friend Jeri just totally bombed her English exam. How do you cheer her up?

   a) Give her a pep talk pronto.
   b) Take her to your kick-boxing class.
   c) Spring for tickets to her favorite band's concert.

7. What's the best way to bond with your buds?

   a) Talk, talk, and talk some more.
   b) Do something fun together, like horseback riding or salsa dancing.
   c) Go on a full-out shopping spree.

8. Your friend just got her first set of wheels. Now what?

   a) You cruise around, listen to the radio, and talk all night long.
   b) You drive to the nearest amusement park and ride every roller coaster at least four times each.
   c) You hit every outlet mall within a fifty-mile radius and hunt for bargains.

To find out what kind of friend you are, count up your As, Bs, and Cs.

Mostly As: Bonding Bud
You and your friends love to talk about anything and everything. In fact, you often have marathon

conversations with pals but never find yourself at a loss for words. Yep—the connection you and your friends share is a deep, emotional one. Just make sure you take a break from the talkfest every now and then to get out and do something wild. That way, you'll *really* have something to talk about!

Mostly Bs: Active Amigo
Talk about a wild child! You and your friends are live-for-the-moment ladies who live life to the fullest, pushing yourself and your friendships to the absolute limits. Life in the fast lane is totally cool as long as you take a breather once in a while. Throw a sleepover to recharge your batteries.

Mostly Cs: Splurging Sista
When it comes to friendship, you are the ultimate Material Girl. You adore shopping with your friends and lavishing your pals with gifts. As long as you realize that you don't have to buy anybody's love, your friendships will be priceless.

4

Unconventional Friends

All friendships are not created equal. Sure, you might have a friend who's *exactly* like you—you're so similar, it's almost scary. But you're bound to have a few friends who couldn't be more different: a rowdy guy pal, the teacher you can always turn to, that chick who's two grades behind you but totally cracks you up. And now, thanks to the 'net, it's even possible to become friends with someone you haven't met face-to-face. Yep, sometimes we find friends where we least expect it—and the most unlikely friendships often turn out to be the strongest. Here is all you need to know about finding and keeping unconventional friendships.

Boy Friends

There's a big difference between a boyfriend and a boy friend. A boyfriend is the guy you crush on. A boy friend is who you turn to for advice about your crush. A boyfriend could potentially break your heart. A boy friend is the one who will help patch it back together. Boy friends are great to have around, especially when you want the famous "guy perspective." They tend to look at things in a totally different way than girls do, so they can help you see everything in a new light. And since guys don't like to gossip as much as girls usually do, you can be sure your secrets are safe with them. They'll give you lots of male attention without any of the usual boyfriend pressures or hassles.

But sometimes when you're good friends with a guy, your feelings eventually run deeper. You get along so great, you wonder what it would be like to date him or (gulp!) kiss him. If he doesn't feel the same about you, however, you could jeopardize the friendship. Trust me, I know. I developed a major crush on my guy friend, Jake, after we'd been friends for about three years. Even though this guy knew every last detail about my life, I suddenly could barely talk around him! It was really intense. I kept my feelings a secret for two months, until one night when I just couldn't take it anymore. I confessed my feelings, but he told me he didn't like me in that way. Things were never the same between us after that. But this doesn't mean you shouldn't share your feelings if you develop a crush on *your* guy friend. Just be sure you're ready to accept the consequences before you fess up.

Family Ties

They say that nobody cares for you as much as your family does. But it's sometimes hard to feel like you're really *friends* with your family members—especially your parents (unless you're a member of the Brady Bunch, that is!). After all, they're the ones in charge of setting rules and curfews. It's their job to make sure you do the right thing and discipline you when you don't. There were tons of times I felt like I *couldn't stand* my mom and dad. But even though we had our disagreements, in many ways my mom was truly my best friend. She cared so much about what happened to me, and she was totally interested in what was going on in my life. That's also the thing that sometimes used to drive me nuts about her (Gawd, Mom, why do you care so much? Get a life!). But I didn't realize then that in some ways I *was* her life. And now that she's passed away, I realize what a gift her concern was and how much I miss it now that it's gone.

Becoming better friends with your mom is easy, and it doesn't take much effort. Start by talking to her. Just tell her what's going on in your life. Even if you think she won't understand, give it a shot. She's been through a lot of the same things you have and will probably be able to give you some insight on what you're going through. Treat her with the same respect you want her to treat you with. Don't call her names or lie to her. You'll gain her trust by earning it first. Give yourself an opportunity to bond by starting Mom-and-Daughter days and sticking to them. You'll feel closer to her once you hang out on a regular basis.

Being friends with your dad is just as rewarding as being friends with your mom, but it sometimes feels tougher to connect. I remember a lot of the times it seemed like my dad didn't know what the heck to say to me once I hit my teens. It was like I had suddenly grown two heads or something. But we always bonded while watching college football on Saturdays, and I have great memories of him trying to teach me how to golf in our backyard. Are you interested in any of your dad's hobbies? Ask him to give you tennis lessons or share his barbecuing secrets. You'll be super-tight in no time!

If you've got siblings, it can be even harder to keep things on friendly terms. There were many times I wanted to wring my little brother's neck, he drove me so crazy! After all, you live under the same roof, so you're competing for bathroom space and phone time. And you're together 24/7, so it's easy to get on each other's nerves. But bonding with your siblings can be simple. Both hooked on *Survivor*? Vow to watch it together every week. Bored out of your gourd? Mix things up by whipping up a culinary creation together in the kitchen and surprising Mom and Dad with dinner. When you're bummed, go to older siblings for advice. If you're hanging with friends, include your younger sibling once in a while. And remember the number-one secret to keeping the peace with siblings: Give one another some space. Don't snoop through your sister's diary or barge in when your bro's on the phone with his girlfriend. If you respect one another's privacy, things will go way more smoothly, and family life will be virtually fight-free.

AIN'T LIFE GRAND?

When it comes to being friends with your family, we can't forget one often-overlooked group: grandparents. Sure, they're older than you . . . but they've done *lots* of living. It may be hard to believe, but they probably have tons of interesting stories to share. A great way to really get to know your grandparents is to interview them. Bring along a list of questions and a tape recorder to record their responses. Ask them about their childhood, their high school graduation, even their first love. You'll be amazed how cool they actually are—guess it runs in the family!

Who's the Boss?

We don't always think of authority figures such as teachers, school counselors, or bosses as potential friends, but they definitely can be. Okay, they're not the type of friends you'd want to have slumber parties or hang at the mall with, but they can be good friends just the same. This sort of friendship is based on mutual respect rather than a mutual love for *Smallville,* and that's okay. We all need lots of different kinds of friends in our lives, and this is one type of pal that can really enrich your life and possibly even shape your future.

Alien Concept #1: Teachers can be your friends. Before you die laughing, hear me out. Teachers get a bad rap. Sure, some of them are crappy—but not *all* of them are. Every school has a few cool teachers who can relate to what you're going through. And contrary to popular belief, most teachers truly care about what happens to you. My high school yearbook adviser was so awesome, and he turned out to be a really great friend to me. I used to come to him for advice on a daily basis—about school, friends, and life in general. He was always willing to listen and steer me in the right direction. In fact, I still keep in touch with him even now, years later. This isn't to say you'll want to be buddy-buddy with all your teachers. You'll naturally click with some and not others. But if you're having a problem with something, consider turning to a teacher you like for help—especially if it's school-related. If you find yourself struggling with a subject or assignment, it's always a good idea to go to your teachers for some assistance. Maybe they'll offer you help with homework or give you an opportunity to earn some extra credit, simply because they know you are truly concerned. After all, you did take the time to come to them personally and talk it out. That shows real maturity, and it will definitely be something that won't be overlooked come report-card time.

Being friends with your boss or manager also has its perks. I'll never forget Amanda, my manager at my part-time job in high school. When I first met her, I thought she was snobby and unapproachable. Frankly, she scared me. But once I opened up to her and treated her like a person instead of a boss, she became like the big sister I never had. She was seven years older than me, so she gave me some really great advice about dating, flirting, and stuff like that. And my job became so much better once I began to bond with her. I was actually excited to go to work. When I needed a day off for something, she was understanding and accommodating since we had a personal relationship. And when the spot for head hostess opened up, she thought of me first. That promotion led to better hours and bigger paychecks. So, in my case, it paid to be friends with the boss—literally! But make sure you don't venture into "brown-noser" territory, because most bosses (and co-workers) can see right through that kind of behavior. Just be genuine, and try to find something to truly like about the person who's in charge.

Once I gave her a chance, I also really liked my school counselor. It felt kind of weird to talk to her at first, until she told me that it was her job to help students just like me. She said that's what she got paid to do, and her multiple degrees on the wall helped assure me that she was qualified. She gave me tons of help when I was having problems at home and offered great advice and guidance once it was time to choose a college. And since everything you tell a counselor is confidential, it was easier to open up to her more than I would have to a friend's mom or someone like that. The next time you need someone to talk to, don't overlook the school counselor. She's there to help.

Most people in authority really care if given the chance. In my case, all I had to do was reach out and ask for support. I urge you to take the leap of faith and do the same. You won't regret it.

The Age Game

Sure, age is just a number—but it definitely matters when it comes to friendship. Have you ever met someone who you thought was totally cool, only to later find out that she was one, two, even three years younger than you are? Or have you ever wanted to be friends with someone who's two or three grades ahead of you? Being friends with someone who's younger or older presents its own set of unique challenges, but they can be conquered with just a little effort and forethought. Listen up.

When you befriend younger people, you get an instant ego boost, because they totally look up to you. In their eyes, you're older, wiser, and way experienced. And you can give them tons of advice, since you've already "been there, done that" when it comes to whatever they're going through. It's a great feeling to help someone who's struggling through the same stuff you've already survived. And maybe your younger pal makes you feel a bit young at heart, too. A chick who's a few grades behind you might be more into board games and amusement parks than crushes and shopping, and it can be refreshing to hang with someone like that sometimes. It helps you remember how you used to be and how far you've come. And it can also be really fun to take a break from your life and sort of "go back in time" for an afternoon or a weekend. Just be careful not to expose your youthful pals to something they're not ready for yet. Use your best judgment here. And be ready to catch some flack from your other friends about befriending someone so much younger. They may not understand why you want to hang with someone like that and start to tease you about it. But that's their problem. If you truly like your younger pal, introduce her to your other friends so they can discover what it is you find so special about her. There's no reason you can't all get along, no matter how wide the age gap.

Hanging with an older crowd also has its pros and cons. Being around older people can make you feel more mature, like you're getting a sneak preview into your future. And older pals can offer you lots of life advice.

But the biggest danger in hanging with people who are much older is that their world might simply be too fast for you. When you're in junior high and high school, the years are like dog years: One year equals about seven years in terms of maturity. So even if someone is only two years older than you, they could be worlds ahead of you in terms of experiences and what they're into. They might be exposed to things like drinking, sex, or drugs, and that is quite likely a realm you're just not ready to enter. This isn't to say you should never be friends with someone who's older, but proceed with caution. Don't do anything you're not ready to do and never rush yourself into anything. Follow your heart.

Write On

Another unique type of friendship is the more out-of-sight variety: cyber friends, pen pals, and long-distance chums. Even though you don't see these friends every day (or *ever*, for that matter), they can still be super supportive and a big part of your daily life.

Thanks to the Internet, you now have the chance to be friends with someone you've never even met in person. Since you don't see these cyber pals face-to-face, chatting with them is like writing in a diary with someone on the other end writing back. These friends won't judge you on your looks or who you hang out with at school and will like you for the "true" you. The only glitch here is that you have to be sure your cyber pals are actually who they say they are. Some forty-year-old men get their thrills by pretending to be a fourteen-year-old girl. Freaks! Make sure you have your parents' permission before starting a cyber friendship. *Never* give out your address or phone number, and never agree to meet the person alone. You can't be too careful!

Pen pals are sort of an old-fashioned concept these days, but they're still around. These are friends you correspond with strictly through the mail. It's so cool to open up your mailbox and find something addressed especially to you. Plus, letters just seem more personal than e-mail. You can send photos, mix tapes, or homemade collages in your packages and keep your pal's letters forever and ever. But since letters can sometimes fall into the wrong hands, never put something in writing that you don't want the whole world to read.

A long-distance friendship can be challenging but totally worth it. My best friend and I haven't lived in the same state for seven years, but we're still as close as ever. We talk at least three times a week, and when I have big news she's the first person I call. We e-mail each other almost daily and send each other lots of cards and letters. Sometimes I even send her videos I make of my life in California. We also stay close by visiting each other at least two times a year. We're living proof that friendships can go the distance—literally! So if a good friend of yours moves away, don't write the friendship off. Instead, *write on*!

When you're in one of these types of "out-of-sight" friendships, the closeness comes not from hanging out on a regular basis but by sharing your emotions and *yourself* from across the miles. If you can find the courage to open up and pour out your heart and soul, the rewards are immense and super-gratifying.

Boyfriend Friends

When you have a boyfriend, you don't just have a relationship with him—you have one with everyone in his life: his family, his friends, even his exes. Obviously, you want his friends and his family to like you. When you win them over, you win *him* over, and your relationship grows even stronger.

When you hang with his friends for the first time, you'll probably be a little nervous. Obviously, they want only the best for him, so you might feel like you're being judged. They're obviously wondering if you're good enough for him. First of all, *you* have to believe you make the cut. Remember: You rule, so there's nothing to be nervous about! Just be yourself. Even though you'll want to impress them, try not to steal the spotlight. No one likes someone who blabbers on endlessly about herself.

Ask his friends lots of questions and try to get to know them. Go with the flow. If they want to go bowling and you don't, be flexible. And never, I repeat *never,* divulge a secret your boyfriend told you to the whole group. If he confided in you that his best friend Joe has been driving him nuts lately, don't ask Joe what his problem is these days. If your boyfriend wants his friends to know a secret, he'll tell them himself. Last, encourage your boyfriend to hang out with his buds, even without you. He had a life before he met you, and you don't want that to stop now. When he hangs with his pals, that will give you a perfect chance to hang out with yours. Everybody will be happy!

When you meet his parents, it can be even more nerve-racking than meeting his friends. You can talk to his pals about the new X-box or the latest Adam Sandler flick, but what are you supposed to talk to his parents about? The weather's always a safe bet, as is your dream college choice. Keep it simple and don't divulge too much information—like how you're dying to get your nose pierced, or how you got a speeding ticket last week. *Less is more.* And be polite. Offer to help out with the dishes or anything else you can. It's best-behavior time! Take a deep breath—it will be okay. Their son adores you, after all—and so will they.

What about his ex? Well, the decision to be friends with her (or not) largely depends on whether or not *he's* friends with her. If they hang out often and are on friendly terms, it's worth trying to get to know her—as long as your jealous streak doesn't kick in. If you feel insecure about it, keep in mind that if they were meant to be together, she'd still be his girlfriend. You've got the spot now, so there's nothing to be worried about. Some ex-girlfriends enjoy trying to stir up trouble between their ex and his new girlie. If she's this type of ex, steer clear. And never tell her anything negative about your boyfriend, even if she tries to pry the info out of you. She'll probably only try using it against you later, and it's none of her business, anyway. If your boyfriend's not on good terms with her, I wouldn't try to be, either. The only exception is if you were already friends with her before you started dating him—'cause *no* guy is worth dumping a friend for, period!

QUIZ
How Open-Minded Are You About Friendship?

1. Your mom tells you she wants to hang out with you on Saturday for a Mother-Daughter Day. You

   a) say okay. It should be fun to hang out with Mom for a change.
   b) agree to go, as long as you go somewhere none of your friends will see you. That would be so embarrassing.

c) refuse. There's no way in hell you're going to spend a Saturday with your *mom.*

2. A guy from your science class asks you if you want to study at the library after school, but you know he has a girlfriend. You

a) agree to go, assuming he just wants to be friends. You can always use another boy bud.

b) ask him if his girlfriend is coming along. That way, he knows that you know he's taken.

c) offer a lame excuse and decline. It's obvious this two-timer wants to cheat on his girlfriend with you, and you're not having it!

3. You just started an after-school job, and your boss is a college chick who seems pretty cool. You

a) ask her all about herself and try to get to know her. She just might become the big sister you've always wanted!

b) act polite to her but follow her lead when it comes to talking about anything personal. You don't want to overstep your bounds.

c) treat her like you would any other boss. You don't like to mix business with pleasure.

4. You're having big problems in Trig, and your dad suggests talking to your teacher about it. You

a) take his advice and vow to talk to the teacher after class. Maybe she can give you some insight that would make a difference.

b) write the teacher a note. You'd feel too weird talking to her face-to-face.

c) tell your dad he's way out of touch. Talking to your teacher about your problems will only make her more aware of your cluelessness.

5. A girl who's two years younger than you moves in next door. You

a) try to befriend her. After all, you know exactly what she's going through.

b) smile at her when you see her outside but keep your distance. You don't want to get all chummy-chummy or anything.

c) avoid her at all costs, because you don't want to risk being seen talking to someone so much younger. Your friends would make fun of you for days!

6. When you're hanging in a chat room online, a girl named Alexis tells you she thinks you're really cool, then asks if she can e-mail you sometime. You

a) give her your e-mail address. It'd be fun to have a cyber pal.

b) say okay but check out her identity further before you tell her anything personal. You can't be too careful.

c) tell her you don't think so. What's the point of striking up a friendship with someone you'll never even meet?

7. After you've been going out with your boyfriend for two months, he asks if you want to get together with his ex-girlfriend for dinner. You

a) happily agree. You've been dying to meet this chick.

b) ask him a few questions about her. You don't want to agree to anything like this until you know all the facts.

c) flat-out refuse. That would just be too weird.

8. Bad news: Your best friend's dad just got transferred to Canada, and they're moving at the end of the summer. You

a) vow to make your friendship work long distance. With e-mail, phone calls, and letters, it will be like she never left!

b) tell her you'll always be best friends but gradually start to hang out with other people. You don't want to feel totally friendless when she leaves.

c) are so bummed, you can barely function. Once your best bud bails, you know your friendship will be dead in the water.

To find out how open-minded you are, count up your As, Bs, and Cs.

Mostly As: Totally Open-Minded
When it comes to friendship, you have no problem thinking out of the box. You know that friendship comes in all shapes and sizes, and you're happy to embrace it in all of its countless forms. You will always have a bevy of interesting pals as a result.

Mostly Bs: Somewhat Open-Minded
It's hard for you to imagine being friends with a family member or someone you met online at first, but you always end up giving it your best shot. Even if it doesn't work out, you gave it a try. And that's all anyone can ask for.

Mostly Cs: Rarely Open-Minded
If your mind were any more closed, you'd have to pry it open with a crowbar! When you think a friendship is doomed (like with a teacher or boss, for instance), you don't even attempt to make it work. But when you effectively end something before it even starts, you are cutting yourself off from many of life's possibilities. Before you give up on a potential friendship, go ahead and give it a try. You'll be happy you did.

5

Best Friends

There's almost no one in the world who's more important to you than your best friend. After all, this is the person you do everything with. She knows you so well, she
can practically complete your sentences. You share
clothes, makeup, and secrets. And she's the one person
you can be around 24/7 and *not* get sick of, even for a
second. Here is everything you need to know about best
friends, including how to pick one, how to *be* one, and
more.

Wanted: Best Friend Forever

Scoping out a best friend can be tricky, because no one
is your best friend on the first meeting. Nope, a best
friendship is built over time. You might be instant
friends with someone you meet at school and have an

immediate connection, but the bond that best friends share is one that's cultivated over months and months of talking on the phone, hanging out, and being there for each other through thick and thin. Even so, you'll probably know right away if someone is best-friend material. How? Best friends are loyal, sweet, devoted, and totally on your wavelength. They make you laugh and capture your interest. When you're with them, you feel great about yourself and about the world. And they "get" you. You don't have to explain yourself to them, because they already know what you're all about. They're genuine and *never* fake. And they always have your back, no matter what. You can count on them for anything.

Sounds pretty great, doesn't it? That's because best friends *are* great. Once you make a best friend, you want to be around that person more than anyone else. Even if you have ten, twenty, or thirty friends, this is the one pal you call first when you've got major news—good or bad. You're the star of your life, and she's your supporting actress, rooting you on from the front lines. She shows you what friendship is all about.

How to Be a Best Friend

Once you've got yourself a best friend, you have to *be* a best friend to keep her in your life. This means being supportive when she's going through a crisis, listening to her obsess over her crush, offering her advice about the perfect outfit or lipstick color, and even helping her cram for her science quiz. Being a best friend is all about being there for the other person 100 percent. But make sure you're getting as much as you're giving. No, this doesn't mean you have to keep score of who does what for whom. But deep down you'll know if she's as there for you as you are for her. This should be relatively equal, or else you'll feel taken advantage of. And no one likes to feel that way.

When you're someone's best friend, she trusts you completely. Don't abuse that trust by badmouthing the person behind her back. There are going to be times when she makes you mad, but resist the urge to bad-mouth her to your other friends. (Even if you swear them to secrecy, that's no guarantee that what you say won't get back to her—trust me!) Instead, write about your feelings in your journal or confide in your mom. Think about how *you'd* feel if she talked about you—'cause that's exactly how she'll feel if you do it to her. Don't take the risk.

Just be the best friend you can be to your best bud. Don't betray her. Follow the Ten Commandments of Good Friendship (page 56) every day, and treat her with the same kindness and respect you want her to treat you with. It's as simple as that.

Secret Code

Your best friend is the one person you tell all your secrets to, and you're the one who hears all of hers. But for a secret to remain a secret, this means you can't tell a soul—no matter how tempted you are to spill the beans. When you promise her you won't say a peep, keep that promise. Your friendship will be the stronger for it.

Of course, you expect the same zipped-lip treatment in return. If you find out your best bud blabbed one of your secrets to someone else (or to everyone in school), you have to call her on it and tell her how much this hurts your feelings. It's hard to trust someone who turns your private thoughts into public information. She'll have to start at square one and earn your trust all over again. Until she does, keep your secrets to yourself.

Be Your Best Friend's Biggest Fan

You should always be your best friend's biggest fan. When she's on the fence about running for class president, tell her she'd be crazy not to go for it, then help her plaster the school with campaign posters. If she's not sure if her new skirt looks okay, assure her that she looks like a total supermodel. When she's freaking over her first date with her crush, be the one who tells her how amazing she is and how lucky he is to have the chance to go out with her. Be the one person in your best friend's life who is always on her side, 24/7. When you're her personal cheer-leader, you'll boost her self-esteem and make her feel like she can do *anything* as long as you're by her side.

Give Me Five!

When you're getting serious with a guy, there are a number of things you can wear—like class rings or letter jackets—to symbolize the strength of your relationship. But when you're best friends with someone, how do you tell the world? Here are five ways to show you're best friends forever.

1. Best-Friends-Forever necklace. Everyone's seen this: two chains with the charm that's a gold heart cracked into two pieces. You wear one half, she wears the other. A classic.

2. Cloned clothes. Okay, you don't want to look *too* Mary Kate and Ashley here, but wearing matching jeans jackets or halters can be a rad way to show everyone you're best friends with *amazing* taste!

3. A single earring. Since you're always there to lend an ear to each other, buy a pair of earrings you both love and split 'em. You wear one, she wears the other. Truly ear-resistable!

4. Matching purses. You're both crazy about Kate Spade, right? Buy matching bags and you'll always look like a stylish team when you strut down the halls or the malls.

5. Dime-store rings. They're cheap, gaudy, and fabulous, and they tell the world you don't need a guy to give you a ring—your best friend is all you need!

What's the Difference Between an Acquaintance and a Best Friend?

Best Friend	Acquaintance
Laughs at all your jokes	Rolls her eyes at your jokes
Knows the name of every crush you've ever had	Sometimes even forgets *your* name
Stays on the phone with you for hours	Doesn't know your number
Trades clothes with you with no complaint	Acts put out when you ask to borrow her skirt
Would never gossip about you	Lives to gossip about you
Helps you with homework	Asks to borrow your homework
Makes you feel like you're #1	Sometimes makes you feel like you don't even rate
Never forgets your birthday	Never remembers your birthday
Would never go after your guy	Loves to flirt with your guy

When Two Becomes Three

You and your best bud are so tight, you're like two peas in a pod. So what happens when one of you makes a new friend and your perfect party of two becomes a sometimes-overcrowded party of three? It's only natural that feelings of jealousy and rivalry would rear their ugly heads in such a situation. After all, you two have shared everything, and now someone new is entering the scene and threatening your tight bond. But a new friendship doesn't have to mean the end of your best friendship. In fact, it can actually make you closer.

I remember when my best friend in ninth grade became friends with a new girl in school. I was so upset! I thought for sure she'd forget all about me. In my mind, I'd been replaced. But that wasn't the case at all. After I freaked out for a few days, I talked to my friend about my feelings. She assured me that I was irreplaceable, then we all began doing things as a threesome. It was totally fun. Now I had *two* great friends instead of just one. Bonus!

If your best bud makes a new friend, try as hard as you can to get to know her. Invite them both to go to the movies with you or have them over for a sleepover. Try not to see her as a threat. You and your best friend share such a special bond, *no one* could break it. Believe in your friendship. For assurance, talk to your best friend about your feelings. I'm sure she'll tell you exactly what I'm telling you now: You rock, and no one can fill your shoes—ever!

If you're the one with the new friend and your best bud is freaking out, try to see things from her perspective. She doesn't want to lose you, and she's worried that this new pal will steal you away. I've been in this situation as well. My best friend went ballistic when I started hanging out with a girl named Laura. She told me I *couldn't* be friends with her because she didn't like her at all. Instead of trying to reason with her and telling her my friendship with Laura wouldn't affect our friendship, I started hanging out with Laura on the sly. It was a really bad situation. My best friend was hurt, and I constantly felt like I was doing something wrong. In the end, we all became friends—but not until we'd shed lots of tears and had tons of fights. Save yourself the pain I experienced by being upfront from the get-go. Tell your friend how much she means to you and try to include her in your plans with your new friend. If you make sure she doesn't feel left out, there should be no hurt feelings. Soon, she'll see that two friends are indeed better than one!

The Bottom Line

I wouldn't trade my best friends for the world. They're the people who have stood by me through thick and thin, who've held my hand through the highs and lows of all life's dramas. But no best friendship is perfect. You'll have fights. You'll hurt each other's feelings. You'll sometimes feel jealous or competitive with one another. But it's all worth it. Because you'll never find anyone more supportive, more loving, more loyal, or more *awesome* than a best friend. Promise.

QUIZ
How Well Do You Know Your Best Friend?

1. What is your best friend's favorite color?

2. What is the name of your best friend's first crush?

3. Who is your best friend crushing on now?

4. What's your best friend's most embarrassing moment?

5. Who does your best friend look up to most?

6. What does your best friend like on her pizza?

7. If your best friend could marry any movie star, who would it be?

8. What's your best friend's favorite TV show?

9. What's your best friend's biggest pet peeve?

10. How many minutes on average does your best friend spend on the phone per day?

11. What's your best friend's favorite school subject?

12. What's your best friend's middle name?

13. Is your best friend a dog or cat person?

14. Does your best friend like mustard or mayonnaise?

15. What's your best friend's allowance per week?

16. What's your best friend's favorite article of clothing?

17. What's your best friend's favorite band?

18. What was the greatest moment of your best friend's life so far?

19. What is your best friend's favorite book?

20. What does your best friend want to be when she grows up?

After your best friend checks your answers to see how many you got right, read on to find out just how well you know your best bud.

14–20: Better Than You Know Yourself
You know so much about your closest pal, it's almost spooky. It's obvious why you're best friends—you're totally on the same wavelength, and you know even the littlest things about her. Continue to nurture your fab friendship and you'll be soulmates for life.

7–13: Not as Well as You Think You Do
Even though you know lots about your best friend, you don't know everything. But that's not necessarily a bad thing. As long as there are new things to discover about each other, your friendship will always be an exciting adventure. Enjoy the journey.

6 or less: You Have a Lot to Learn
You sure don't know much about your best friend. This either means (a) you haven't been best friends

for that long or (b) you're not a very good listener. In either case, you really should make an effort to get to know her better. How? Ask her about her life and truly listen to her responses. Discover what really makes her tick. Once you do, your best friendship will be even better.

6

Fight the Good Fight

No matter how good your friendship is, you're going to fight eventually. You are such a big part of each other's lives, it's inevitable that at one point you're going to clash over something. But a fight doesn't have to mean the end of the friendship. In fact, resolving a rift can actually make your friendship stronger. And it's way healthier to get something that's bugging you out in the open and deal with it than to brush it under the rug and pretend it doesn't exist. Here's all you need to know to fight the good fight.

When a Friend Ticks You Off

You're supposed to meet a friend at the mall at 5:00, and she's still not there by 5:30. You're furious. When she finally arrives (full of lame excuses), what should you do? You've got three choices:

a) Tell her exactly how you feel—no holds barred.

b) Downplay your feelings by telling her you're kind of mad, but it's no big deal.

c) Smile and say nothing.

What's best? In situations such as these, honesty really is the best policy. If you're truly friends, you owe it to *both* of you to tell it like it is. It can be scary to tell someone you're mad at her, but if you don't, you're essentially telling her that her bad behavior is okay with you. And you're bound to feel resentful if you're being treated like dirt but never get the chance to say something about it. Plus, she won't get the chance to make it up to you if she

---

Fighting No-nos

When you're in a fight, always stay away from the CHIN. No, I'm not talking about the body part here. CHIN is an acronym for the four things you should never do in a fight, no matter how mad you are. The next time you're in a knock-down, drag-out, *never*

Cuss

Hit

Insult

Name-call

No matter what!

has no idea you're mad. Afraid of conflict? Don't worry: If you're close pals, getting mad or even staying that way for a few days won't mean the end of any friendship.

How to Fight Fair

Before you have a blowout, have a realistic idea of what it is that you want and what you think the other person wants. For example, you want your friend to show up when she says she will, and you think she wants to take her own sweet time. Then tell the person how you feel without attacking her or name-calling. Go into specifics: How does it make you feel when she's so tardy? (Maybe you're worried about her at first, then mad that she has so little regard for you or your time.) When she tells you why she's been late the last five times you've gotten together, listen without getting defensive. Then try to come to a resolution that suits both of you. Maybe she'll set her watch fifteen minutes early or you'll make your mall dates fifteen minutes later. You'll bring a book so you'll have something to do in case she gets held up; she'll have to pay for the movie if she's over fifteen minutes late. Come up with a decision you *both* can live with.

In a perfect world, this is how all fights would go down. But of course not all arguments are resolved this easily. Sometimes friends stay mad at each other for days or weeks. A friend may decide to give you the silent treatment or completely go off on you for no reason. Or you might just be too afraid to tell a friend that you're mad. Here are the top worst fighting tactics and how to combat them.

1. The Silent Treatment

If someone isn't a good communicator, she might "punish" friends by giving them the silent treatment instead of telling them why she's mad. But this won't solve anything. Nothing will be resolved until you talk things out. If a friend is giving you the silent treatment, go up to her and say, "Listen, I know you're not talking to me right now, but I'd really like to work things out. Can we talk for a few minutes?" Hopefully, your attempt to reach out will be successful. If you're the one giving the silent treatment to someone else, cut it out and speak up. Once you tell her why you're mad, she can apologize and make it up to you. But she's not a mind reader. You have to tell her why you're mad if you want her to do something about it.

2. Kicking and Screaming

Sometimes when you try to talk something out with a friend, she becomes extremely defensive and just completely goes off on you—calling you names, screaming, yelling, just going crazy. If a friend acts like this toward you, calmly say, "Listen, you're obviously really upset right now. Let's just take a break and talk tomorrow.

Once we cool down, we can really think things through." If she won't listen, leave. You don't need to take any kind of verbal abuse. If you're the one who's going off, take a deep breath and just get out of there for a while. Yelling and screaming won't solve your problem—it will only add to it.

3. Acting Mad Without Saying Why

Sometimes a friend who is mad will just act angry without telling you why. She'll "forget" to return your calls, stop sitting by you in the caf, or blow off plans with you for no reason. When you ask her what's wrong, she acts like you're the one who's crazy: *"Nothing's wrong! Why do you ask?"* If you think you know why she's mad at you, say so. Tell her, "Listen, I know I screwed up when I _____. I'm really sorry. I'd like to talk it out with you, but I wish you'd tell me how you feel about it." This might make her open up. If she still denies she's mad (or you have no idea *why* she is), ask her why she's been blowing you off or avoiding you. Tell her you really miss her friendship and would like things to be the way they used to be. Open up a dialogue and really talk things out.

If you're the one who's acting mad but not saying why, just gather your courage and tell the person straight-up what's been bugging you. This passive-aggressive game you're playing will only wear you both out, so why bother? Instead, just be direct and address the problem head-on. That way, you can reach some sort of resolution and quit wasting your time and energy on it.

4. Feeling Too Scared to Say Something

Maybe you're truly mad at someone but just too freaked to say something about it. If this is the case, think of it this way: If you *don't* say something, you are cheating yourself in a major way. Your friendship can't grow stronger until you work this out, so you owe it to yourself (and your friendship) to speak up. To work up your nerve, practice what you're going to say in front of a mirror or write it down. Tell your mom about what's going on and practice your speech on her. Once you know what you're going to say and how you're going to say it, you'll be way less nervous once you actually do voice your feelings.

5. Ganging Up on Someone with Another Friend

This is a common scenario, especially when you have two best friends. One of them gets mad at you, then calls the other one. She takes your friend's side. Now, they're *both* mad at you. Or you get mad at one friend, then recruit another pal to join in the fight. Now, you're not so alone—and you have someone to dis her with. This situation sucks, whether you're the ganger or the gangee. But, depending which side you're on, you'll have to handle the situations differently.

If you're the one who's being ganged up on, it can feel really lonely. It seems like the whole world is against you. Sit your friends down and tell them you're really hurt over what's happened and would like to work it out. Tell them you're not sure why Friend #2 even got involved in the first place, but you'd like to resolve things with both of them. If you feel you can't get a word in edgewise, consider meeting with the two friends separately. Or if a "big talk" is just too heavy, invite them both over for a sleepover so you can work things out over popcorn and Chris Klein flicks.

If you're ganging up on another friend, think about how you'd feel in her shoes. Is it really necessary to get the other friend involved? Try to work things out with her one-on-one. If that isn't possible, ask all of the friends who are involved over to your house. Order a pizza and hash things out. Once you're all in the same room and everything is out in the open, the she-said/she-said game ends, and you can work toward a peaceful resolution.

6. Transmitting Mixed Signals

A friend is mad at you, but she tells a mutual friend instead of you. Or you're mad at your best friend, and you tell an acquaintance about it in hopes that she'll pass the info along. This is known as "indirect communication," and it rarely works. When you tell someone something in hopes she'll tell someone else, the message almost always gets screwed up in the translation. Plus, her feelings will likely be way more hurt when she hears you're mad second- or third-hand. It's much better to go to the source and just let her know why you're peeved.

If you've heard that someone's mad at you through the grapevine, resist the urge to tell the mutual friend how you feel in hopes it will get back to your peeved pal. Instead, just go up to your friend and say, "Listen, I heard from so-and-so that you're mad at me, and I'd really like to work things out." Just be direct. That way, you can work things out instead of wasting time passing messages from one person to another.

7. Sending an Angry E-mail or Note

When you're mad at someone, it's sometimes easier to write it in an e-mail or a note than to address the problem face-to-face. But if you receive an e-mail like this, don't write back. Why? Because when you're not communicating directly with someone, it's so easy to say things you don't mean. Instead, call the person or go over to their house. Tell them you got their note and you'd like to work things out.

If you have sent an angry e-mail to someone but haven't heard back, give the person a call. I've ended two major friendships through letters and e-mails, and I ended up regretting it. Too many things were left unsaid.

Pick up the phone and hash things out with your friend in a direct manner. That way, you'll have no regrets down the line.

8. Not Forgiving and Forgetting

Maybe a pal has told you she's sorry a zillion times, but you just can't seem to forgive and forget. Or you're the one doing the apologizing, but your friend is still holding a grudge. Sometimes "I'm sorry" just doesn't cut it, especially when someone's trust has been violated.

If you can't forgive, tell yourself that the friendship will probably never be exactly the same, but it *can* be good again. Let your friend earn back your trust. Assuming she is truly sorry, she'll probably do whatever she can to win you over again.

A friend of mine once wrote a mean note about me to someone else, and I found it. I was so hurt. I confronted her, and she apologized. But I just couldn't forgive her. I kept hearing the words of that note over and over again in my head. This went on for over a year. Even though she tried to make it up to me, I wanted nothing to do with her. I was too mad. But then I realized I was wasting way too much energy being angry. The hatred I felt for her was wiping me out, literally. I was tired. I had relived this nightmare every day for over a year, and it was time to let it go. I knew she was truly sorry. Although I doubted we'd ever be as close again, I told her I'd like to rebuild our friendship. It didn't happen overnight, but little by little we eventually became tight once more.

If your friend won't forgive you, do whatever you can to win back her trust. When you say you're going to do something, do it. When you tell her you're going to be somewhere, be there. Let your actions speak louder than your words. Show her that you're loyal and dependable and that you're worthy of her trust.

9. Having a Fist Fight

Some people feel they have to resort to physical violence to display their anger. This won't solve a thing. So if someone tells you they want you to meet them at the bike racks after school to duke it out, tell them no way. If you're having a fight with someone and they raise their hands at you, get out of there fast. If you feel you're in real danger, call a teacher, your parents, or even 9-1-1. Trading punches isn't the answer!

10. Using Guns, Knives, or Other Weapons

I wish I didn't have to mention this one, but in the age of gang wars and Columbine, it's a reality that has to be addressed. If someone tries to pull a gun or a knife on you, get the heck out of there. Call 9-1-1. Do whatever you have to do to protect your safety. In this case, how you react could mean the difference between life and death.

Envy Among Friends

When you're good friends with someone, you'll proba-bly feel jealous or competitive at one time or another. Maybe she got a boyfriend before you did and you're green with envy. Or you're secretly dying to get a higher score than she does on the SATs. Competitiveness and jealousy among friends is a totally natural thing and nothing to feel ashamed of or weird about.

You're together so much, it's only natural you'll feel competitive once in a while. If you're both on the bas-ketball team, you might have a friendly rivalry over who can score more points in a particular game. This is harm-less fun and can actually drive you both to do better. But if your competitiveness is consuming you and all you can think of is beating your friend at sports or school, it's time to analyze why one-upping her is so important to you. Why do you feel you have to be better than she? Maybe you've got some insecurities of your own you need to deal with. Once you figure out why you're so competitive with the person, it's much easier to turn your competitiveness around and eventually grow from the experience.

It's the same with jealousy. It can either be a tool for destruction or a great gift, depending on what you do with it. If you're jealous of a friend, first analyze what you're jealous of. Maybe you're both trying to lose weight and she just shed ten pounds. Instead of feeling resentful, get motivated! Ask her how she lost the weight and ask if she'll help you follow her lead. When you admit to yourself that you're envious and what you're envious of, you can use it as a goal-setting measure. If you're jealous that your friend has a boyfriend, ask her to set you up with one of her b-friend's pals. Instead of being bitter about her happiness, take charge and find some of your own!

But what happens when you're jealous of something that's beyond your control? Maybe you're jealous that you're friend's 5'11", but you're only 5'2". Obviously, no amount of goal-setting will help you grow nine inches. But you can think about why you're so envious of her height. Maybe you were always teased about being the shortest kid in the class, and you're still insecure about it. I bet if you talk to your friend about your envy, she'll confess she's always wished she were shorter. Use your envy as a motivator to explore your feelings and talk things out.

If your friend is envious or jealous of you, there are steps you can take to ease her pain. First, don't gloat. If you made the soccer team and she didn't, don't talk about it 24/7. If you've noticed she's been treating you differently lately, confront her. Tell her you'd like the chance to air this out so it doesn't come between you. Next, offer to help her get some success of her own. Encourage her without being patronizing, then tell her you're there for her completely. And be sure to hang out lots with your pal during her low point. People who are envious of their friends often fear they're going to be abandoned. So spend some time with her and let her know her friendship is still very important to you.

Making Up

After you've resolved a fight or dispute, it's time to make up. But this can be a little awkward. After all, you've just had a knock-down, drag-out, and you're both still feeling a little wounded. Here are six ways to make up in style.

1. Share a banana split.

Sometimes ice cream is an absolute cure-all, and this is one of those times. And sharing the same sundae represents the fact that you're sharing and caring again. So grab two spoons and dig in!

2. Have a burial ceremony.

Write down what your fight was about on a piece of paper, then bury the paper in your backyard. Talk about burying the hatchet!

3. Hug.

After a fight, a hug is a great way to erase the tension. A little cheesy, but it works!

4. Invite her to spend the night.

You've been through a lot, and now it's time to bond again. Eat junk food, stay up too late, and tell each other everything. By the next day, your fight will be a distant memory.

5. Go see a chick flick.

Nothing brings two girls closer together more than laughing and crying over the latest girl movie. Bring a box of Kleenex, buy a jumbo popcorn, and lose yourselves in the sappy story.

6. Sign a peace treaty.

Write up a paragraph that says you'll try to never fight again, then both sign it. The next time you get in a tiff, pull out the piece of paper for an instant tension-breaker.

When You Can't Kiss and Make Up

Since all arguments are not created equal, sometimes a fight is just too major to resolve. Check out the "Friends Fallout" chapter (pages 195–206) for tips on how to deal when your rift is irreparable.

The Last Word

No one likes to fight (except for maybe Mike Tyson), but all friends have it out at one time or another. You and your friends are all individuals with their own unique sets of opinions, and you're going to clash at some point.

But, as I've explained, conflict can actually make you closer when it's handled in the right way. So the next time you're mad about something, say it loud and say it proud. Your friendship will be the better for it.

QUIZ
What's Your Fighting Style?

1. You and your best friend were supposed to go to a movie Friday night, but at the last minute she bagged on your plans. You

    a) say nothing, holding your anger inside.

    b) tell her she really hurt your feelings.

    c) scream that she's totally inconsiderate, then hang up on her in a huff.

2. Your dad told you he would raise your allowance if you helped more around the house. But once you pitch in, he refuses to give you more cash. You

    a) decide you're not going to talk to him for a few days.

    b) calmly tell him that you're really disappointed he went back on his word.

    c) freak out and scream that he's the meanest dad in the world.

3. After you delivered what you thought was a decent oral report in speech class, your teacher gave you a D+. What do you do?

a) Shoot her dirty looks the rest of the semester.

b) Talk to her after class about her unfair grading practices.

c) Go to the principal to try to get her fired.

4. You heard through the grapevine that a guy in your history class has been spreading nasty rumors about you around school. You

a) go out of your way *not* to talk to him.

b) ask him what his problem is.

c) pour a chocolate milkshake over his head in the middle of the cafeteria.

5. You're babysitting to earn a little extra cash, but the kid you're watching is a total brat. When he decides to squirt mustard into your new purse, you

a) grab the bag from him, turn up the TV, and try to ignore his immature antics.

b) tell him that's not a very nice thing to do, then ask why he did such a thing.

c) squirt ketchup all over his Nintendo.

6. Your snobby cousin is over for a visit, and she just told you the zit on your chin looks like Mt. Everest. Your response?

a) Silence. Why stoop to her level?

b) "I don't know why you feel the need to be so rude to me."

c) "Oh, really? Well, your butt's so big, it deserves its own zip code!"

7. You're slaving away at your part-time job when your boss gripes you out for giving a customer the wrong change. But the thing is, you didn't even wait on that customer. You

a) roll your eyes and sigh deeply.
b) tell her that she's mad at the wrong person.
c) scream, "You're so unfair!" then stomp off.

8. You're talking to your boyfriend on the phone about something really important, but you hear his TV on in the background. It's obvious he's watching the show and tuning you out. You tell him

a) you've got to go.
b) he's being super inconsiderate and you don't appreciate it.
c) he's the biggest jerk alive and there's no way you're taking a backseat to ESPN!

Tally up your totals to find out your fighting style.

Mostly As: Silent but Deadly
When you're mad at somebody, you don't say a thing. Instead, you rely on the silent treatment to get your point across. The only problem with this tactic is that you never get to say what you really want to

say. Maybe you're worried that if you say something, you'll ruin the relationship. But *not* saying something is way more damaging because you never have a chance to resolve anything. Try *speaking up* instead of *clamming up* the next time you're mad. You'll feel so much better.

Mostly Bs: Calm, Cool, and Collected

If somebody makes you angry, you don't go ballistic or seethe in silence. Instead, you tell them how you're feeling in the most direct way possible. If they hurt your feelings or let you down, you simply say so. Way to go, girl! It takes guts and maturity to say what you mean without resorting to name-calling or put-downs. That's totally the way to be.

Mostly Cs: Kicking and Screaming

You don't just tell somebody you're mad, you show them—by screaming, yelling, slamming doors, and freaking out. Your fights are more like temper tantrums—but once they're over, you feel like a load has been lifted off your shoulders. You get two points for not holding in your feelings, but maybe you should try cooling off before you blow up. The next time you're about to explode, count to twenty before you say anything or go outside and get some air. If you can talk to someone rather than scream at them, you'll get way better results. That's a fact.

7

Communication Nation

You communicate with your friends on a daily basis—writing them notes, calling them on the phone, talking to them at school. But is your message really getting through? Knowing how to communicate *effectively* is a valuable life skill, but it's one that's a mystery to most people. After all, there are no "Communicating with Your Friends" classes at your school, right? Well, I think there should be! That's why I've gathered up my very best communication tips and am offering them up as a crash course in communications. Stop, listen, and learn!

Communication 101

How many times have you told your friend something, but she thought you meant something else? It's happened to me at least a million times. No matter how hard I try to be direct and straightforward, I still manage to send mixed signals or get my wires crossed every once in a while. I'll never forget the time I told my best friend I thought her new boyfriend was really cute. I meant it as a compliment to her (translation: "You have great taste in guys!"), but she thought I meant I wanted him for myself. When she started acting kind of weird toward me, I had no idea why. After a few days of pouting, she finally fessed up, and we worked it out. But that just goes to show you how easily a friend (even your *best* friend!) can think you mean one thing when you really mean another. How can you make sure you get your intended point across every time? Here are my Top Ten Rules of Communication.

TOP TEN RULES OF COMMUNICATION

1. Say what you mean, and mean what you say.

This is a simple rule, but it's not always so simple to follow. It's sometimes way easier to beat around the bush and hope the person clues in to what you're saying. But why leave this to chance? When you say what you mean, you'll know for sure your message is coming through in the exact way you intended. What a relief!

2. Cut out the sarcasm.

Everyone has used sarcasm to get a point across at one time or another. A friend asks you for help on her homework for about the zillionth time in a row, but she never offers to help you with hers. You're peeved. But instead of telling her to do her own homework, you say, "I should start charging tutoring fees, since I'm obviously Miss Brain of the Universe who has all the right answers!" Your friend laughs uncomfortably, not sure if you're kidding or not. You hope she gets the message that you're sick of helping her. But unless you say it without the sarcasm, you'll never know if she gets your meaning or not.

3. Don't drop hints people can't catch.

It's Wednesday, and you decide you want to do something with your friend on Friday night. But instead of just asking her if she wants to get together, you say, "I'm going to be really bored this weekend. I have nothing to do!" No response. Then, the next day, you say, "I hope there's something good on TV tomorrow, because I'm going to be home all night. How lame!" She smiles and says nothing. On Friday morning, you finally decide to ask her if she wants to spend the night that evening. She says, "I can't—I made plans to go to the movies with my family. You kept talking about staying home this weekend, so I didn't think you wanted to do anything!" The lesson here? You might think the clues you're dropping are totally clear, but that's not always the case. Never rely on subtle hints to get your message across.

4. If someone asks you if you're mad at her, tell the truth.

You're mad at your pal, so you're acting all aloof and standoffish. She comes up to you and says, "Are you mad at me or something? You're acting kind of weird." Your response: "Oh no, I'm not mad. I have no idea what you're talking about!" She walks off, wondering what the deal is, and you continue acting mad for a few more days until your angry feelings subside. Bad move! It would have been a lot easier on everyone if you'd just told her the truth and gotten it over with instead of harboring bad feelings that will never be fully resolved. If someone asks you if you're mad, that means she really wants to know. So let her have it!

5. Know when honesty isn't the best policy.

Yes, lying is a bad thing. But if your friend asks you if her new haircut looks okay and it looks like she stuck her finger in a light socket, it's time to get creative. Saying something like, "Wow, it looks totally unique. *Nobody* else has hair like that!" allows you to be nice without telling a bold-faced lie. Sparing your friend's feelings takes priority over telling the whole truth in this case. Afterwards, you can always go shopping for cool barrettes and headbands to salvage her style.

6. Give your friends equal airtime.

Since your problems are happening to *you*, they're your number-one concern. But your friend feels the same way about her problems. So if you talk 24/7 about what's going on in your life, she won't think you care about what's going on in hers. Give her an equal opportunity to talk, obsess, and vent—or else she'll tune out on your problems forever.

7. Don't ask for advice unless you really want it.

You ask your friend if you should dump your boyfriend after he stands you up for the third time in a row. She tells you that you should lose that loser pronto! You stay with him anyway, then get mad at your pal for calling him a loser. What's wrong with this picture? You asked for her opinion, then got mad at her for giving it to you. That's just not fair. Don't ask for something unless you can really take it.

8. If you hear a rumor, go straight to the source.

If you heard from a friend-of-a-friend that so-and-so said something about you, don't get mad until you go to so-and-so for her side of the story. See, a lot of times people get mad over things that were never actually said about them in the first place. It's best to go to the source *before* you go ballistic.

9. If a friend is taking advantage of you, speak up.

You are getting so sick of your friend bumming rides from you without ever offering you any gas money. But day after day you pick her up and drop her off without saying a word. How is she supposed to know you're mad unless you say something about it? As the old saying goes: "The first time it happened, shame on her. The second time it happened, shame on *you*." People can only take advantage of you if you let them. So say something and stop being a doormat!

10. When you have to, tell friends things they don't want to hear.

Let's say you've noticed your friend is partying too much and skipping a lot of school. Should you say something, even if you think she'll get mad? Yes. You need to tell her you're concerned, even if you fear she'll be annoyed. Sometimes you have to say the one thing friends don't want to hear, because that's the thing they need to hear most.

There you have it—my top ten rules of communication. Follow them, and you'll nix mixed signals *forever*!

Phone Home

Alexander Graham Bell rules. What would you do without his amazing invention, the telephone? After all, it's your lifeline, connecting you to friends, acquaintances, classmates, and crushes. But even an amazing creation such as the phone comes with its problems. Here are the most common telephone troubles and how to solve them when they come a-calling.

CALLER ID A friend calls *way* too much.

THE SOLUTION If you don't want to tell her straight-out that her constant calls are totally annoying, you can always tell her your parents are putting a limit to your phone time and you can only receive calls from, say, five to six. Or the first time she calls, tell her, "I've got a lot to do tonight, so I'll talk to you tomorrow." Another option: "Listen, my dad's expecting an important call tonight, so could you e-mail me instead?" Once you give her some boundaries, she'll probably chill.

CALLER ID Your friend never calls you back.

THE SOLUTION It's so rude when you call someone and she doesn't call you back. But before you freak, give her the benefit of the doubt. Maybe she didn't get your message. If it's been more than a day and you still haven't heard from her, give her another call. If you *still* don't hear back, ask her what the deal is the next time you see her in person. Just be upfront: "Hey, girl, what's up with you not calling me back?" When you put her on the spot, she'll probably feel really bad and promise never, ever to do it again.

CALLER ID You run out of things to say.

THE SOLUTION Sometimes, awkward silences abound on the phone even when you're talking to a good friend. What do you say when there's nothing left to say? You can always ask weird, random questions—like "If you were an animal, which one would you be?"—to keep someone on their toes. Or if all else fails, pretend you're Oprah and your pal is your interview subject. Start asking questions . . . *lots* of questions. Since people love to talk about themselves, you'll never run out of things to say. Or, if the silence lasts too long, just cut the conversation short. Chances are your talk tomorrow will go much better.

CALLER ID Your parents say you're on the phone too much with your friends.

THE SOLUTION When your parents freak about your phone time, try to come up with a compromise that suits everyone. Do they want you to limit your calls to fifteen minutes apiece? If you'd be happier with twenty, have a pow-wow to see if you can reach a peaceful solution. Once you do, compensate for your non-phone time by sending e-mails or writing notes instead.

CALLER ID A friend left you an embarrassing message on your answering machine.

THE SOLUTION Your pal Jill just left a message about how she heard you made out with your crush last weekend, and then *your dad* overheard it. How mortifying! First, try to smooth things over with Dad. ("She's only kidding . . . whoa, that Jill is such a prankster!") Then call Jill and tell her that you'd rather not have your tonsil-hockey episode made public knowledge among your entire family. Having Mom or Dad record your outgoing message will remind your pals that it's a family answering machine, not your own personal loveline.

You've Got Mail

E-mail is an awesome way to communicate. You can IM your friends, chat with them in chat rooms, or send them personal messages whenever your heart desires. Sometimes it's easier to express yourself online than it is on the phone. Just make sure you never tell a friend something online that you wouldn't tell her face-to-face. E-mailing someone can fill you with a false sense of bravery, like, "I'm going to write an e-mail and tell her off!" But the minute you hit "send," you might be full of remorse. Why? Because the things you send in cyberspace still have real-life consequences. Remember that before you send something you'll regret.

If you're online 24/7, your parents may be concerned.

If they insist you turn off the computer and join the real world, take their advice. The time you spend on the computer is time you *aren't* spending doing homework, hanging out with your friends, or pursuing your hobbies. This doesn't mean you should stop surfing the 'Net altogether, but just do it in moderation.

Taking Notes

Writing notes to friends is a fab way to stay connected. Just make sure you're not writing notes when you're supposed to be taking notes in class! You might miss some valuable info, or even be humiliated by a teacher

Amazing Acronyms

Here are some letters you absolutely need to know to write the perfect note:

BFF	Best Friends Forever
WBS	Write Back Soon
SSS	Sorry So Short (or Sorry So Sloppy)
LYLAS	Love Ya Like a Sis
TTFN	Ta Ta For Now
YGG	You go, girl!
LOL	Laugh out loud
ROFL	Rolling on floor laughing

who decides to read your note aloud (gulp!). For that reason, never put anything that's top secret in writing. You never know whose hands the note might land in! If you must write something private, use a secret code that's difficult to crack. Otherwise, your classified information could become front-page news in no time.

Turn the Page

If you have a pager or a two-way, you've probably encountered your own set of communication problems. The number-one pager complaint I've heard is when someone pages you 9-1-1 but her message is not at all urgent. You drop everything, find a pay phone, invest the thirty-five cents to call her, then find out she simply wants fashion advice. Urgh! What to do? Jokingly say, "I didn't realize that figuring out what outfit to wear tonight rates as an emergency!" Or give her a code of her own: "Listen, when you have an urgent—but non-emergency message, type in 247 . . . that's our code, 'cause you're my best bud 24/7!" That way, she feels flattered, not battered.

One Last Thing

Whether you're talking, dishing, venting, obsessing, ranting, or raving (or all of the above!), the way you talk to your friends is so important. It's *everything*. Because if you weren't able to talk to your compadres, it'd be a mighty lonely, lonely world. So always say what you have to say in the best possible way you can say it. Hopefully, your message will get through with no problem. But if you encounter some static, hang up and try again. And again. And again.

QUIZ
How in Touch Are You and Your Friends?

1. Your best friend is trying on a pair of pants at the mall that don't do a thing for her. When she asks you how they look, you say

    a) "They look okay, but I bet we can find a pair that looks even better."
    b) "Ohmigosh—you look like a fat cow!"
    c) "They look really cute! You should definitely buy them!"

2. Your pal wants to tell you about her latest crush. When she says she's soooooo in love with him, you say

    a) "Tell me all about him! I want to hear every last detail!"
    b) "He's definitely cool. Does he have any cute friends?"
    c) "I'm soooooooooo in love with my guy, too. Don't you think he's hot?"

3. You ask your friend if you should dump your boyfriend. She says you definitely should because he's a real jerk. You

   a) appreciate her honesty. At least she had the nerve to tell you what she really thinks.

   b) feel a little peeved she put down your boyfriend but try not to hold it against her.

   c) are furious at her for calling him a jerk. *She's the jerk!*

4. Your pal Sara asks you to help her with her history homework. The thing is, you've helped her with her homework every night this week, and she *never* helps you with yours. You

   a) tell her you'd be happy to help her with history if she'll assist you with algebra.

   b) tell her you can't study tonight because you've got other plans.

   c) go ahead and help her without telling her you're mad.

5. Your friend Kerri calls you 24/7, but she never has anything to say. What do you do?

   a) Ask her to chill on the phone calls.

   b) Tell her your parents are ragging you for using the phone too much.

   c) Don't answer the phone when you see her number on Caller ID.

6. You're on the phone with your best friend when your boyfriend beeps in on Call Waiting. You

a) tell your boyfriend you'll have to call him back.

b) see what your boyfriend wants and then take the call that seems more important.

c) tell your best friend you'll have to call her back.

7. If you get a message on your machine from your friend and she says it's *urgent,* how long does it take you to call her back?

a) Five minutes or less

b) An hour or two

c) A day or longer

8. An acquaintance sends you an e-mail asking advice about a guy problem. You

a) e-mail her your best advice as soon as you can.

b) think over her problem for a day, then e-mail her back.

c) forward her e-mail to all of your friends to get *their* opinions.

How in touch are you and your friends? Count up your As, Bs, and Cs to find out.

Mostly As: Totally in Touch
You're a Communication Queen! Not only do you always get your point across, you do it in the nicest way possible. That means knowing when to tell it like it is but also realizing when honesty isn't necessarily the best policy. Keep up the good work!

Mostly Bs: Occasional Mixed Signals
You and your friends communicate fine most of the time, but sometimes you miss the mark. It's no biggie, 'cause everybody sticks their foot in their mouth sometimes. Just think about what you're going to say *before* you say it, and you'll see instant interaction improvements.

Mostly Cs: Always Out of Touch
Your communicating rating is lower than low. Sure, you and your friends are doing a lot of talking—but is your message really getting through? It's time to look at how you interact with others and give your conversational skills an overhaul. Study my Top Ten Rules of Communication (pages 116–120) and try to follow them. Once you do, you'll finally truly be heard.

8

Love and Friendship

A friendship can undergo some big changes once a cute boy enters the picture. Maybe you've got a boyfriend, and your friend feels left out. Or your best friend just hooked up with a cutie, and you're the one feeling left behind. A romantic relationship can change the dynamics of a friendship in a major way, but if you take the right steps, your friendship can survive—and thrive!—even when love is in the air.

Love Changes Things

When you get a boyfriend, your life changes bigtime. But your friends' lives experience some aftershocks as well. You used to hang out with them every weekend; now you're spending loads of time with your boyfriend. They used to be the first person you call with big news; now you dial *his* digits. It's hard for friends *not* to feel left out and a little bit abandoned when a new guy enters the picture. But you can help them feel less deserted by taking a few simple steps. First, never blow off your friends for your boyfriend. I have been guilty of this myself, but it's *so* not worth it.

Your boyfriend should enhance your life but not *become* your life. You had friends when you met him, and you should have friends even after you commit. This means calling your friends often and making an effort to include them when you can. Set aside at least one night a week to hang with your girlies, and *never* break these plans to be with your guy. Let your friends know that they're still important to you, even though you've got a new guy in your life. Show them how much you care on a daily basis.

When your friend gets a boyfriend and you're the one who feels cast aside, it can be a helpless feeling. Suddenly, the friendship you've counted on for so long is totally different, and it seems like there's nothing you can do about it. But there is. First, tell your friend how you're feeling. Assure her that you're happy for her, but tell her you miss her a little bit, too.

Set up a Girls' Night Out on a weekly basis. That way, you know you'll stay connected. If she's hesitant, tell her it will be a great opportunity for her guy to miss her—and that's a good thing! Invite her and her boyfriend along on group outings to the movies or the mall. This will give you a chance to see your friend *and* get to know her boyfriend. And cut your friend some slack—at least at first. At the beginning of any relationship, couples go through a "honeymoon period" where they want to be around each other every waking moment. This stage usually lasts about two to three months. If you must, wait it out until your friend enters the real world again. This doesn't mean you should tolerate her totally ignoring you or treating you like a doormat. But if she talks about her guy nonstop or doesn't call you as much as she used to, give her a break. When you get a new boyfriend, hopefully she'll do the same for you.

Relationship Rescue

Sometimes the troubles that romantic relationships bring to a friendship are much more major than a friend blowing you off or hanging with you less. If you hate her new boyfriend or she hates yours, this can cause a rift between friends that's irreparable. So what should you do if you detest your friend's dude?

First, try to see the good in him. Almost everybody has at least one quality that's likable. Once you find his, focus on that when you're around him. If he's standoffish but totally smart, try to focus on his "smart" side by challenging him to trivia contests or engaging him in heated debates over current affairs. Second, keep in mind that your friend really likes him. If you truly hate him, that will only hurt her—so maybe keeping your feelings to yourself is in your best interest. (An exception to this rule is if he's abusive or endangers her safety in any way. See "When a Friend Is Abused," pages 135–136.) Last, try killing him with kindness, especially if your feelings of hatred are mutual. It will be hard for him to dislike someone who's so sweet to him. And, if you play nice long enough, you just might trick your mind into believing you actually *do* like him.

Another common boy/bud dilemma is when you and your friend both like the same guy. This happened to my friend Heidi and me when we both started crushing on a cutie named Chris. Since we knew we'd ruin our friendship if we both went after him, we decided that neither one should pursue him. Our friendship was worth more than any crush would ever be! Another time I had a thing for a guy named Gage. It turns out he didn't like me back, but he *did* like my friend. She asked me if it would be okay if she went out with him. Even though I felt a little weird about it, I said sure. And they're still together—seven years later! The moral to this story? There are no set rules here. While it's not the best idea to crush on the same guy or date a friend's ex, sometimes it can work out if you talk it over with your friend first. If you can reach a mutual decision on how to proceed, make your move from there. But if you want to go out with him and she's not cool with it, think twice about doing it. No guy is worth losing a friend over.

Obviously, it goes without saying that you should never go after your friend's boyfriend while she's still dating him. But you already knew that, right? Right!

When a Friend Is Abused

If your friend is being abused physically, emotionally, or sexually by her boyfriend, she might not have the nerve to tell you directly. Here are some of the warning signs to look out for.

Her boyfriend:
- harms her physically in any way—including pushing, slapping, kicking, or shoving.
- frequently humiliates her or puts her down.
- tries to control her by telling her what to wear and dictating who she can and can't hang out with.
- threatens to harm her physically if she leaves him.
- forces her to have sex even if she says no.
- demands to know where she is at all times.
- is overly jealous and possessive.

Your friend:
- has unexplained bruises, scratches, or broken bones.
- feels guilty or ashamed for no apparent reason.
- keeps secrets from you and won't answer your questions directly.

- never wants to hang out anymore.
- withdraws from her own family.
- skips school and social events.
- gives you lame excuses that make little or no sense.
- always seems like she's walking on egg shells around her boyfriend in fear of making him angry.

If you suspect your friend is being abused, let her know that you're concerned and that you care. Listen to her without judging her. Above all, stress the fact that this is not her fault. Her boyfriend probably makes her feel like she "deserves" his abuse, but she doesn't. She is not a bad person—her boyfriend is, and he needs professional help. Encourage her to get help immediately from a parent or guidance counselor, then contact the National Domestic Violence Hotline at 1-800-333-SAFE for support. If her life is in danger, call 9-1-1. Don't wait until it's too late.

Friends and Dating

An ideal way to mix friendship and dating is to go on a double date. That way, you get to hang with your pals *and* your boyfriend at the same time! Double dates can be a blast, especially if you do something interactive that everyone can enjoy, like going miniature golfing or bowling. You can play guys against girlies or couple against couple—and the loser buys the winner frozen yogurt afterwards! (The worst double date is the movies, because you're movie-watching and not talking to each other, which is the whole idea.)

The coolest thing about double dates is that you have an ally, so you're a lot less nervous. And when there are four people on the date, there are no awkward silences. Plus, you always have someone to go to the ladies room with to gab about your guy.

Maybe you have a b-friend and your pal doesn't, so you're tempted to set her up with one of your boyfriend's friends. I've played Cupid many times. Sometimes it works out; sometimes it doesn't. Just don't pressure your friend into doing anything she doesn't want to do. If she's up for the set-up, fine. But if she isn't, don't bug her about it. Follow *her* lead. Once she agrees to the set-up, suggest a double date. That way, it will be way less awkward for everyone, and if she doesn't end up liking him, she'll at least have you to talk to.

If a friend wants to set you up, be open to the possibilities. Even if you don't hit it off with the guy, it'll be an experience. And who knows? He might just be the coolest guy you've ever met. You'll never know unless you take a chance. But if the date doesn't work out, don't hold it against your friend. She only had your best interests at heart.

Valentine's Friend-Fest

Don't have a date for Valentine's? *So what!* When you indulge in one of the following amigo activities, you'll feel nothing but love on V-Day.

1. Host a "Love Yourself" dinner. Load every dish with heavy garlic, since you won't have to worry about smooching anyone later. Then go around the table and make each guest say three things they love about themselves. Love-o-Rama!

2. Throw a "Stupid Cupid" sleepover. Rent girl-power movies—like *Thelma and Louise, 28 Days,* and *Charlie's Angels*—that make you glad you don't have a boyfriend to deal with. Celebrate your singledom in style!

3. Deposit dime-store Valentines into all your friend's lockers and slip Hershey's kisses into their pockets when they're not looking.

4. It's Red Day. What's that mean? You and your pals wear all red to school. Eat red food at lunch: cherry soda, tomato soup, red peppers dipped in salsa, and strawberries drizzled in raspberry preserves. Blare a vintage Simply Red CD on the car stereo on your way home. Then cap off the evening by renting *The Red Balloon.*

5. Honor St. Valentine by inviting your friends over for mud masques and virgin margaritas. While other girls are dressing and stressing, you're maxing and relaxing with mud on your face and friends by your side. Before you know it, you'll be in exfoliation ecstasy. What a feeling!

Breaking Up Is Hard to Do

Another time boys come into play in a friendship is during a breakup. When your friend breaks up with a guy, it can be the most devastating time in her life. She needs you now more than ever. But surviving a friend's breakup isn't always easy. She'll lean on you so much for so many things, it can wear you out fast. If you follow the following ten rules, however, you'll breeze through the breakup with no problem.

1. Be willing to listen to the same story over and over again.

She'll want to tell you how he broke up with her, what he said, what she said, and what she should have said at least a million times. Each time, you have to listen as if it's the first time you're hearing it. Telling her story is an important part of the healing process, so let her tell her story again and again.

2. Tell her how much she rules.

When this guy left, he took her self-esteem with him. She feels lower than low. You need to convince her how cool she really is. She is the best, and you have to tell her *why* she's the best.

3. Tell her how lame he is for letting her go.

He made the biggest mistake of his life when he let someone as cool as your friend go. Tell her that over and over again. Repeat: "He's going to regret it someday. But by then it will be too late, because you'll have someone way better."

4. Don't tell her you always thought he was a loser.

Even if you always hated this guy from the get-go and saw this breakup coming since day one, don't tell her this now. The "I told you so" trip is only going to make her feel worse, so keep it to yourself.

5. Distract her from thinking about him.

Take her to the movies. Make her go dancing. Force her to go to the mall. She won't feel like getting out, but it's your duty to make her do just that. The more active she is, the less she'll think about him and the sooner she'll move on.

6. Convince her not to call him.

At least once after her breakup, she'll probably really, really want to dial his digits. But it's your job to persuade her this is a bad idea. She'll only regret it afterward. He is not worth her time or energy anymore. If anyone should be making a call, *he* should be calling *her*. Tell her not to give him the satisfaction!

7. Always come prepared.

When needed, a good friend will provide the breakup-ee with: Kleenex, ice cream, waterproof mascara, and lots and lots of hugs.

8. Always change the station when "their song" comes on.

You don't want to expose her to "their song," "their movie," "their restaurant," or anything else starting with "their." It will only cause her pain, and that's what you're trying to avoid here.

9. Just be there.

Depending on her mood, she'll want to scream, cry, talk, groan, whine, vent, or be silent. You need to be there, no matter what. She needs to know she can count on you.

10. Convince her that she will survive this.

Tell her there are way better guys out there, she obviously wasn't meant to be with this one, and what doesn't kill us makes us stronger. (Whew—what a mouthful!) Play "Survivor" by Destiny's Child for her, and tell her it's her theme song. With your help, she's going to make it!

When you go through a breakup of your own, lean on your friends for this kind of support. Your friends *want* to be there for you. Let them give you the special treatment and TLC that you give them day after day. That's what friends are for.

The Bottom Line

I hope by now you've learned that boys and friendship *do* mix. You don't have to choose one over the other. Too many girls blow off their friends for their boyfriends, and this is just not cool. Friends are just as important (if not more so) than any guy will ever be. So cherish your pals as much as you cherish your guy. Love comes in many shapes and sizes, and the love of a friend is something that's special and spectacular. Don't trash it, *treasure* it.

QUIZ
Do You Believe Romance and Friendship Can Mix?

1. You just met a guy you're totally into, and—yippee!—he likes you back! When your friend says she's worried she'll see you less, you

    a) assure her she'll see you just as much. You're not going to give up your girlies for some guy!

    b) tell her she might see you a little less, but you'll still go out at least once a week.

    c) tell her she's probably right. You want to be with your guy 24/7!

2. Your best friend just got her first major boyfriend. How do you feel?

    a) You're totally happy for her. If she's happy, you're happy.

b) You're glad she found someone she likes but kind of worried it will affect your friendship.

c) You're so jealous you can barely see straight. You'll *never* see her now!

3. The guy your friend is dating is a world-class jerk. You absolutely *hate* him. You

a) try to find something to like about him.

b) avoid him at all costs.

c) tell her she should break up with him immediately.

4. Your new boyfriend is constantly fighting with your friend, Hillary. They can't see eye to eye on anything. You

a) try to encourage them to get along.

b) see them separately but never together.

c) decide to see Hillary less.

5. You and your pal Patricia are both crushing hard on the same guy. What do you do?

a) Agree that you should both forget him. That way, there won't be any hurt feelings.

b) Ask him who he likes best. If he likes her, you'll bow out gracefully.

c) Go after him full-force. You're going to win his affections if it kills you!

6. Your friend is dating a guy who's totally nice, smart, and cute. He's so perfect, you're starting to wonder if *you* like him. You

   a) push the thought out of your head. He's off limits.
   b) allow yourself to secretly fantasize what it would be like to date him but never take it further than that.
   c) flirt shamelessly with him every chance you get.

7. Your boyfriend has a really cool pal you think would be perfect for your best bud. The trouble is, she doesn't want to be set up. What's your next move?

   a) You throw a party to see if they'll hit it off in a group setting.
   b) You keep asking her if she's had a change of heart. If you bug her enough about it, maybe she'll change her mind.
   c) You invite them both to the movies and trick them into going on an involuntary ambush date.

8. Your bud just called and told you her boyfriend of two years just dumped her—three days before Prom! You

   a) drop everything and head over to her house. She needs a shoulder to cry on.

b) tell her you're really sorry, then ask if there's anything you can do.

c) say she's better off without a lame-o like that. In fact, you've *always* thought he was a moron.

Do you think romance and friendship mix? For the answer, count your As, Bs, and Cs.

Mostly As: No Doubt, Scout
Romance and friendship absolutely mix in your book—so beautifully, in fact, they make a delicious Love Pie! Your friends are important to you whether you and your pals have boyfriends or not. It doesn't make one bit of difference either way. When a boyfriend enters the scene, that's just one more person you can hang out with and get to know. There's more than enough love to go around!

Mostly Bs: Maybe, Baby
Love and friendship don't *always* mix, but you believe they can. It just takes a little work sometimes. When your best friend meets a new boyfriend, you might go through a temporary adjustment period where you miss your bud's 100 percent attention. But once you get to know her guy, you're totally cool with the situation. Once you give it a chance, it's all good.

Mostly Cs: No Way, José

When you or one of your pals gets a boyfriend, your friendships are in major trouble. That's because you just don't feel that friendship and love can co-exist—and, as long as you have that attitude, you're probably right. Time for a reality check! Friendship does change a bit when love enters the picture, but it doesn't have to come to a screeching halt. If you devote equal time to your friends *and* your boyfriends, life will be fuller than you'd ever imagined.

9

Party Time

When you're together with your friends, you want to have fun. But even the most ingenious of girls will run out of ideas on occasion. That's where this chapter comes in handy. You'll find tons of inspired gift ideas, party themes, and games you can play. Don't have a reason to celebrate? You'll find loads of those, too. So put on your party hat and get ready to *par-tay*!

Wrap It Up

It's your friend's birthday and you don't have a clue what to get her. Even worse, you're strapped for cash. But never fear. You don't have to have a lot of money to get a killer gift. You just have to have a little creativity—and if you don't have any of that, you're in luck, 'cause I've got some to spare!

One thing I often do for friends' birthdays is come up with a cheap theme gift. For my friend Una's eighteenth birthday, I decided to go with a beach theme since she's a total surfer chick. I gave her ocean-scented candles, yummy-smelling sunscreen, a big straw hat, some fab sunglasses, and the Red Hot Chili Peppers' "Californication" CD in a basket. Then I wrote a little poem to tie the whole gift together: "You're a surfer goddess / the queen of the sea and the pool / hope you have the best birthday ever / because you totally rule! Happy Birthday!" Okay, so I'm not much of a poet—but it doesn't matter. When you create a theme gift for somebody, it shows that you think they're worth the time and effort. And that's worth more than any amount of money in the world.

A homemade gift is also a great way to show somebody you care. Making your friend a collage commemorating everywhere you've gone together using pictures, ticket stubs, menus, and matchbook covers is a unique way to honor your friendship. Other cool creations include a beaded necklace, a watercolor painting, or a homemade batch of her favorite double-chocolate-chip cookies. When it's made by you, she'll know the gift comes from the heart.

Yet another cool gift idea is the "Friendship Coupon." When you present her with one of these, you offer her the gift of your own special services. If you give killer manicures, offer her a year's worth of pedicures and manicures. If you're the makeup queen, volunteer your makeover expertise. Or if you're notorious for choosing movies she hates, let her pick the next five movies you see *without* griping about it. Homemade coupons such as these are truly priceless.

Hip Happenings

Want to jazz up your party? It's easy when you plan it around a cool theme. Here are five bashes that won't blow.

- THE THEME: Fave Rave

  THE DEAL: Everybody has to bring their favorite movie of all time, and you watch them one after the other.

  THE REFRESHMENTS: Snack-bar food—popcorn, soft drinks, and nachos

  THE INVITATION: A jumbo-sized movie ticket

  THE PARTY FAVOR: A box of Jujyfruits

- THE THEME: Scrapbook-o-Rama

  THE DEAL: Guests bring their favorite pictures and a blank scrapbook, and you all create mementos that will last a lifetime.

  THE REFRESHMENTS: Food that brings back memories, like mac-and-cheese, juice boxes, and S'mores

  THE INVITATION: A scrapbook-style design full of favorite photos and special souvenirs

  THE PARTY FAVOR: A disposable camera

- THE THEME: Makeover Madness

  THE DEAL: Everyone is required to bring their entire cosmetic inventory—foundation, mascara, lipstick, *the works!*

  THE REFRESHMENTS: Glam, model food like organic veggies, fresh fruit, and imported bottled water

  THE INVITATION: A compact with the details written in paint pen on the mirror

  PARTY FAVOR: Fake eyelashes

- THE THEME: Costume Kaboom

  THE DEAL: Each guest must dress as their favorite TV character

  THE REFRESHMENTS: Couch potato snacks such as corn chips, soft drinks, and pints of ice cream

  THE INVITATION: A remote-control-shaped message.

  THE PARTY FAVOR: A TV Guide

- THE THEME: Fab Fiesta

  THE DEAL: Since it's a Mexican-inspired party, everyone must wear Mexican-inspired outfits: pretty embroidered dresses with sombreros.

  THE REFRESHMENTS: Think south of the border—tacos, quesadillas, and enchiladas

  THE INVITATION: A colorful maraca with fiesta facts written on its handle.

  THE PARTY FAVOR: A piñata

Mind Games

A party just isn't a party unless there are games involved. But since you're a bit old for Pin the Tail on the Donkey, which games should you break out? Truth or Dare is a tried-and-true favorite. You can watch your friends squirm while you ask them if they've ever told you a lie, then see them turn ten shades of red when you dare them to call their crush. (But never dare them to do something dangerous, or anything Tom Green would do!) If the party is co-ed, Spin the Bottle is a retro game that's coming back in a major way. The premise: You sit in a circle and spin a bottle. Whoever the bottle is pointing to when it stops is who you have to smooch—whether you want to or not! Both of these games are oldies but goodies for a reason: They're fun, entertaining, and *never* go out of style.

My friend Eliz's favorite party game is called "Celebrity." You split into two teams and make sure you have two watches with second hands. Then each party guest writes down five celebrities on small slips of paper. (For instance, mine would be A. J. McLean, Madonna, Usher, Katie Holmes, and Jason Biggs—one celebrity per page, and the more obscure the better.) You put all of the folded slips of paper into a hat. One person on your team has sixty seconds to describe as many of these celebs to your team as she can. Say I draw "Faith Hill." I say, "She's a country singer, married to Tim McGraw, her big hit was 'Breathe.'" Someone guesses Faith Hill, and I set that slip of paper in our pile. Then I draw again, and I'm on to the next celeb. When describing your celebrity, you can never say "rhymes with _____" or "starts with the letter __." Once my sixty seconds are up, someone from the other team gets sixty seconds. You keep trading off like that until all the celebs are guessed correctly. Once that happens, you count up your team's slips of paper to see which one wins. It is truly a total blast!

Thanks to the latest game-show craze, you can always flip on the tube and play along with whatever game show is on. Or you can tape several shows over the course of a few weeks and watch them all night long. Whoever gets the most questions right wins a silly prize, like green nail polish or a bottle of bubbles.

When you're brainstorming for game ideas, remember the object is to just have fun. As long as your guests are having a good time, it doesn't really matter *what* you do. And sometimes the cheesiest, corniest games are the ones that make you laugh the loudest in the end.

Girls' Night Out

Going out with the girls is so important. That's why I challenge you to set aside one night a week for "Girls' Night Out." My girlfriends and I have been getting

Happy Days

Since the major holidays come a little too infrequently for my taste, I decided to come up with a few special days of my own. Here are three reasons to blow your party horn and go a little crazy.

NOVEMBER 28 BLACK FRIDAY

Celebrate the biggest shopping day of the year with a night of catalog-browsing and Home-Shopping-Network-watching. Top off the party by saluting shopping queens past and present: Deborah Foreman in *Valley Girl* and Alicia Silverstone in *Clueless*.

JANUARY 8 ELVIS'S BIRTHDAY

Fry up a peanut-butter-and-nanner sandwich, throw on your bell-bottoms, and crank "Jailhouse Rock" to commemorate the day the King entered the world. And don't forget to rent *Honeymoon in Vegas* (for the totally out-there flying Elvis scene).

SEPTEMBER 14 TRL'S FIRST APPEARANCE

Obsess over cuter-than-cute Carson, listen to your favorite boy band CDs, and host an MTV marathon to commemorate the debut of the rulingest TV show ever. I hope this show never retires!

together every Saturday for as long as I can remember. Sometimes we hit a club and dance all night; other times, we stay in and paint one another's toes. But one thing we always do without fail is bond like crazy. We catch up on one another's lives, then talk about everything under the sun—our hopes, dreams, likes, dislikes, boyfriends, and exes. And our big rule is that we don't break our plans for anyone or anything. Girls' Night is totally sacred. *No boys allowed!*

Since I've started setting aside this time for the girls, my friendships are much more solid. It's something I look forward to all week long. In fact, some of my fondest memories are of these Saturdays I devoted to the girls— and I'm sure there are many more to come. So go ahead— get out there and make some memories of your own!

Savor Each Day

There just aren't that many reasons to celebrate in this world. That's why I believe when one comes along, you should really go all out. Always make the effort to make your holidays and friends' birthdays special. When you can have a party, go for it. Treasure your weekends and your private time. And try to make the time you spend with your friends a genuine celebration. When you get down to it, life's little moments are what truly matter. Make yours count.

QUIZ
What's Your Party-Girl Persona?

1. Your good friend Lucy, an avid snowboarder, is having a birthday next week. What do you get her?

   a) A huge assortment of snow globes to commemorate her favorite sport

   b) A vintage *I Love Lucy* lunchbox (since, of course, *you* love Lucy!)

   c) A gift certificate to her favorite store

2. It's your grandparents' wedding anniversary, and you want to go all out. What do you do?

   a) Throw them a big party and invite everyone they know.

   b) Ask a few of their friends to join you for a barbeque at your house.

   c) Take them out to their favorite restaurant.

3. It's Friday night, and you don't have any plans. What do you do?

   a) Call up every person you know and ask them to meet you at the bowling alley for a last-minute bowl-o-rama.

   b) Invite your five closest friends over for a slumber party.

   c) Ask your best friend if she wants to catch a movie.

4. It's your birthday. You walk in your front door and hear "Surprise!" Yep, your best friend has thrown you a surprise party. You feel

   a) totally psyched. You love being the most popular girl in the room!

   b) shocked, but happy. You can't believe she went to all this trouble.

   c) embarrassed and a little bit mad. You hate being the center of attention.

5. When you're hanging with a few friends at your house, someone suggests you play "Truth or Dare." You

   a) are all for it. Let the games begin!

   b) are hesitant at first but finally agree. Maybe it will be fun.

   c) say no way. You don't want to risk being dared to do something you don't want to do.

6. Your friend Jenni suggests making every Saturday a "girls-only" night. What's your response?

   a) Okay, as long as you do something wild. Otherwise, a boy-free night will be too boring.

   b) Maybe. It might be fun once in a while—but every single Saturday seems a bit extreme.

   c) Sure! You'd love the chance to bond with your girlies.

7. Your friend called and said her cousin, who lives in the next town over, is having a huge Halloween bash that night. Do you want to go?

    a) Of course. If there's a party, you're there.

    b) Maybe. It sounds okay, as long as your friend stays by your side.

    c) Nope. You hate going to parties where you won't know anyone.

8. What's your dream party situation?

    a) A big, crazy bash that lasts all night long.

    b) A makeover party with ten of your closest pals.

    c) A sleepover with your two best friends.

What's your Party-Girl Persona? Count up your As, Bs, and Cs to find out.

Mostly As: Wild Child
You're into huge, out-of-control gatherings—the bigger the better. What's the point of getting together with a handful of friends when you can get together with a *hundred* friends? Just make sure you take a moment to connect with your pals, or they'll feel lost in the shuffle. Once you've given them a few minutes of one-on-one attention, you're free to do what you do best: mingle.

Mostly Bs: Social Sista
Your perfect party consists of ten guests or less. Why? That's big enough to feel like a bona fide bash, yet small enough to allow you to talk to every single person in the room. Plus, you're not likely to get any visits from the cops for disturbing the peace. That's always a plus.

Mostly Cs: Bond Babe
Big parties aren't your thing. They're loud, messy, and full of rowdy revelry. Who needs it? You'd rather hang with one or two of your closest pals. That way, you can really bond with the people who mean the most to you. That's totally cool, as long as you hit a big party or two now and then. If you don't mix things up, you'll never know what you're missing.

10

That's What Friends Are For

It's not always going to be fun and games with your friends. At some point, a friend of yours is going to go through a crisis and will need you more than ever. I'll never forget the way my friends came through for me after my mom died, stopping by and calling me every single day. Or how much my friend Shawn needed my support when he came out of the closet to his parents and was so scared. But I'll also never forget how insensitive my ex-friend Maura was after my beloved cat J.D. died. When she laughed at me for acting so "stupid" over a "dumb cat," our friendship abruptly ended at a time I needed her most. How you treat your own friends during a life crisis will likely make or break your bond. This chapter tells you how to handle many of the pitfalls and turning points I've experienced in my own friendships. I sincerely hope it will help you cope with the ones you encounter in yours.

Love Her to Death

When someone your friend loves dies—be it a parent, grandparent, or family pet—it is hard to know how to react, especially if you've never gone through a loss like that yourself. But this is a time when your friend really needs to know you care. Even if you don't know what to say, say *something.* Tell her you're there for her. Let her know how sorry you are that she's going through this. Ask how she's feeling. When my mom died, a few of my so-called best friends fell off the face of the earth, and it hurt me deeply. When I confronted them later about it, they told me they didn't know what to say, so they just left me alone. But the fact that they weren't there for me hurt so much worse than their saying the wrong thing ever could have.

When a friend is going through the loss of someone she loves, she's been let down by the world and slapped in the face by the fact that life is so not fair. Don't add to her pain by letting her down, too. Just be there to listen. Buy her funny little gifts. Send cards. Bake cookies. Drop by for no reason. Be a friend in the truest sense of the word. And don't harp on trivial matters of your own. I remember the night when my mom was having surgery to remove her malignant tumor, my friend Laura called and said, "Oh, I'm going out clubbing tonight. I can't wait! What are you doing?" That hurt, because she was obviously so insensitive to my situation. On the contrary, my friend Traci called and said, "I'm canceling my plans and coming over to talk. I'm not taking no for an answer!" That's what I needed to hear. When a friend is going through a major crisis like this, she needs you to set aside your own problems and plans to be there for her. She doesn't need to hear about your crush or your date this Saturday. Her pain overshadows all that. Acknowledge it and help her deal with it. If she's crying or screaming in anger, never tell her to calm down. This is all part of her healing process.

The one sentiment you should avoid at all costs is this: "If there's anything I can do, let me know." Your friend is too upset to let you know anything. She'll never call and say, "I need you to bring me a pint of Ben & Jerry's" or "Bring over the latest Ben Stiller vid so we can laugh over something silly," but she needs you to do these things all the same. You just have to take the initiative and do them without her asking you to. As the saying goes, "The smallest good deed is better than the grandest good intention."

After a death, depression is perfectly normal. But if you start getting worried that your friend is clinically depressed, check out these warning signs:

Feeling sad or down in the dumps

Eating more or less than usual

Difficulty sleeping or a desire to sleep all the time

Avoiding friends and family

Crying

Feelings of hopelessness

Skipping school

Negative outlook on everything

No interest in the future

Diminished interest in hobbies

Thoughts of death or suicide

If any of these symptoms persist for more than two weeks, something's wrong. Your friend needs help.

Depression Confession

If your friend has been acting down lately—crying a lot, avoiding your calls, sleeping all the time—she might be depressed. You're probably worried that she's going to tell you to mind your own business if you talk to her about it, but she needs to know you're concerned. Ask her how she's feeling, and then really listen to her response. Don't try to fix what's wrong—just hear her out. She might need to cry about her feelings for a while. She needs to be around someone who will hear her out without making fun of her or judging her.

So even if she's told you the saga of her breakup a zil-lion times, don't tune her out. She needs to talk about it, and you—being the fab friend you are—need to listen. After all, she really needs you—and you'll probably need her to return the favor someday.

If your friend mentions suicide, even in a joking way, take her very seriously. Tell someone who can help, like a parent, counselor, or doctor. Even if you promise her you won't tell anyone, you should seek help for her. There's nothing more devastating than when a suicidal person confesses to a friend who doesn't say anything—only to have that person attempt suicide or, even worse, succeed.

Bottom line: Take your friend's depression seriously, no matter what. Mentioning suicide is a cry for help . . . even if she makes you swear not to tell anyone. Keeping this info to yourself could cost your friend her life. Call the Nine Line at 1-800-999-9999 for more info.

When Parents Split Up

If a pal's parents are getting divorced, she really needs your support. Divorce brings about a huge amount of change for the entire family, and it can be totally confus-ing for the teens involved. Your friend might be suddenly thrust into the middle of a custody battle or forced to uproot everything and move. She may be feeling anger, sadness, or guilt about the situation. Or perhaps she feels she's to blame for her parents' divorce, even if it's not true. If her parents fought a lot, she might even be feeling relieved that they're splitting up—but then she'll probably feel guilty for feeling that way. A divorce brings on so many mixed emotions. She'll need you to help her sort them out.

The most important thing you can do for your friend right now is to simply be there for her. Listen. Let her spend the night at your house if she needs to get away from the situation for a few hours. Remind her that her parents are divorcing each other, not her.

If your parents are divorced, you can offer her some insight, since you've probably experienced many of the same things she's going through. But this doesn't mean you can't offer support and encouragement if your parents are happily married. No matter what your situation is, you can let your friend know that you care.

Experts say the first year after a divorce is the toughest on the entire family. If you notice your friend is having an especially hard time or displaying any of the depression symptoms listed above, suggest she talk to a teacher or school counselor. There *is* help available.

Coming Out

When a friend is coming out of the closet, he or she may be feeling really freaked that *you're* going to freak. But the fear of how friends will react is eventually out-weighed by the desire to create open and honest relationships with those closest to them. I'll never forget how nervous my friend Shawn was to tell me he was gay. Since I'd known him to be "straight" all through high school, he didn't know how I was going to react to the news that he liked boys. But I took the news very well. Even though my mom had always said she wished Shawn and I would get together, I'd had a sneaking suspicion he was gay all along. I just tried to be completely supportive and treat him the same as I always had.

If a friend comes out to you, don't judge them or tell them it's "gross." And never criticize them for being different. I believe homosexuals were born gay. If you're straight, it's always been natural for you to like guys, right? Well, that's how they feel, too. This is natural for them. If you feel weird around your friend at first, don't worry: This is totally normal. You're adjusting to this new side of them, and it can take some time. Just listen to what your friend is going through. Be there for her as she tells her parents. Ask her about her latest crush. Treat the person the same as you would any other friend.

One worry some girls have is that their lesbian friend is going to fall for them. Just because she likes girls doesn't mean she likes *all* girls, just as you're not crushing on every guy in the world. So relax, already!

When your friend comes out to you, respect her

boundaries. She might not want you to tell anyone. Abide by her wishes. If your pal experiences discrimination of any kind, stand up for her. She needs your support right now.

One of my best friends is gay. He's Will and I'm Grace. We love each other deeply. Just because you have different sexual preferences doesn't mean you can't be amazingly close friends. As long as you allow your pal to choose his or her own lifestyle *without* judging it, you'll be a-okay.

For more info on this topic, check out the Parents and Friends of Lesbians and Gays (PFLAG) Web site at www.pflag.org. It's awesome.

When Partying Becomes a Problem

When you suspect a friend has a drinking or drug problem, it can be really hard to know how to proceed. You're not her mom, so you don't want to be bossy and tell her what to do. But at the same time you really care for her and don't want to see any harm come to her. Sometimes being a good friend means you have to intervene. To get better, your friend will have to admit she needs help. But you can be the one who encourages her to get the help she needs.

How can you tell if your friend really has a drinking or drug problem? It can be tough, because most people do all they can to hide these problems. But there are some warning signs to look out for. If you see one or more of the following warning signs, your friend may have a problem:

- Says she can quit any time she wants to, but never does
- Has been drinking or taking drugs way more than usual
- Drinks to get drunk
- Tries to solve problems by drinking
- Drinks at inappropriate times—before driving, going to class, or during homework
- Harms herself or others
- Passes out after drinking or doing drugs
- Spends lots of time thinking or talking about getting drunk or high
- Frequently says she's going to quit cold turkey, or switch from liquor to beer
- Undergoes a major personality change when under the influence
- Doesn't remember things that happened the night before, or "blacks out"
- Lies about how much she's had to drink or how many drugs she's done—or denies it altogether
- Blows you off to get drunk or high
- Gives up hobbies and starts slacking on homework

- Drops old friends and starts hanging with the stoner crowd
- Hides bottles of alcohol and often drinks alone
- Has to drink more and more to get drunk
- Doesn't think you can have fun without getting drunk or high
- Often has major hangovers
- Pressures everyone around her to get drunk and "party" with her
- Becomes promiscuous on drugs or alcohol
- Feels tired and depressed
- Talks about suicide
- Has been suspended or arrested for an alcohol- or drug-related incident.

If your friend is displaying any of these warning signs, you need to talk to her about it. Whether or not she takes your advice is her decision, but you need to speak up. If you're scared to approach her alone, ask a mutual friend who's also concerned to join you. It's a good idea to talk to someone like a teacher or counselor *before* you talk to your friend. You don't have to mention your friend by name, but talk generally about the problem and ask them what the best steps are for you to take. That way, you'll feel more prepared for the conversation.

When you decide to talk to her, make sure she's not drunk or high. She needs to be clear-headed for this conversation. Start by telling her you're worried about her. Speak in an understanding tone of voice, without pity or judgment. Don't preach, blame, or criticize. No matter how horribly she's been acting, she's not a horrible person. She might very well have a disease that's causing her to act this way. Avoid sermons, lectures, or verbal attacks.

Be specific when you talk and focus on the facts. Bring up incidents such as "You left the party without me, and I had no idea where you went," instead of "You are so undependable." Tell your friend what you've seen her do when she's drinking or using other drugs. Then tell her how you feel, because she can't argue with your feelings. Tell her how it feels for you to see her drunk or high, but never call her an alcoholic or a drug addict. You're not a doctor, so you can't diagnose her. Just tell your friend you want to help.

But don't be shocked if she gets angry with you, says she doesn't want your help, or denies having a problem altogether. This is a common reaction among drug-and-alcohol abusers. She might blame others for the problem or give excuses for why she drinks or uses other drugs. This defensiveness has nothing to do with you. Your only option is to take a few steps back and let her know you'll be there for her. Your concern just might spark her recovery at some point. But don't feel guilty. You've done all you can, and you can't *make* someone get help if they don't want to.

If she says she wants help, offer to go with her to AA, talk to her parents, or meet with the school counselor. This will show your friend you truly care. Ask her what she is going to do about her problem and what kinds of support she needs from you to stop or limit her drinking or drug using. Be as supportive as possible in encouraging her to follow through. Then get some help for yourself. Your friend isn't the only person who needs support in this situation. You might feel lonely and stressed. You've probably worried yourself sick over your friend's behavior and its possible consequences. It's important that you talk about your feelings. You can see your school counselor, or check out groups such as Al-Anon or Alateen that help friends and families of alcoholics deal with their emotions. (For more information, call 800-344-2666.)

Dying to Be Thin

In this world of stick-thin models and actresses, weight is a major concern for many girls. Dieting is an American obsession. But sometimes harmless dieting transforms into a deadly eating disorder. Anorexics and bulimics are totally consumed with thoughts about food and weight. They think about it all the time. When you have a friend who suffers from an eating disorder, it can be really scary.

Is she going to die from it, like seventies singer Karen Carpenter did? What should you do to help?

First, check out the following warning signs. If your friend is displaying one or more of these, it's highly likely that she has a problem.

ANOREXIA WARNING SIGNS

- Preoccupied with food and weight loss
- Has a distorted body image—for example, she thinks she looks fat even if she is too thin
- Compulsively exercises to work off calories
- Spends less time with friends and stops pursuing hobbies
- Only eats certain foods, like celery sticks or dry baked potatoes, and is highly restrictive in her diet
- Moves food around plate but never eats
- Avoids going out to eat
- Denies being hungry or offers excuses for not eating
- Weighs herself many times a day and freaks out when she gains half a pound
- Stops having her period
- Is often cold
- Loses her hair
- Has yellow, sallow skin and looks malnourished

BULIMIA WARNING SIGNS

- Preoccupied with food and weight loss
- Has a distorted body image—for example, she thinks she looks fat even if she is too thin
- Compulsively exercises to work off calories
- Spends less time with friends and stops pursuing hobbies
- Binges and purges—eats tons of food in one sitting, then throws up
- Throws up several times a day
- Looks "dazed" or glassy-eyed after purging
- Goes to bathroom a lot after meals
- Smells like vomit
- Takes laxatives
- Has stained or discolored teeth
- Has calluses on her hands and knuckles

If you suspect your friend has an eating disorder, you need to talk to her about it. Mention her eating habits, but don't focus on her appearance or tell her she looks too skinny. She is so focused on her appearance already, this tactic will only backfire. Instead, say, "You never join us for pizza" or "You always go to the bathroom after meals." Be specific. She might deny her behavior, but just stress the fact that you're concerned. Don't be surprised if she gets defensive. There's a lot of shame that comes along with an eating disorder, so she'll probably deny her behavior or tell you you're blowing it out of proportion. Focus on her feelings. Say things like, "It seems like you get really nervous before lunch. Why are you so worried?" Listen without being judgmental. Encourage her to get help by saying, "Maybe you should talk to someone about this stuff that's bugging you. I think the school counselor could really help." But never tell her to eat more or less. If she thinks you're trying to control her or tell her what to do, this will make her feel out of control. When she feels out of control, she leans on her eating disorder for a sense of power. It's a vicious cycle, and one that can be deadly.

Don't be surprised if she doesn't get help after just one talk. You'll probably need to talk to her and listen to her many times before she'll feel safe enough to tell you what's really going on. If your friend continues to have problems but won't admit them to you, talk with a parent or counselor to see what can be done. Or contact the American Anorexia and Bulimia Association at 212-575-6200. Your friend needs help. When she finally gets it, she'll really need your support. No eating disorder is cured overnight. She'll need your encouragement as she struggles to overcome hers.

Cutting Edge

Self-mutilation or self-injury is when people cut or burn themselves to deal with difficult feelings that build up inside. It's become more common over the past few years and can be deadly when untreated.

If you think a friend is self-injuring, you need to do what you can to help. Here are the warning signs:

- Having unexplained frequent injuries, including cuts and burns
- Making excuses for being so accident-prone
- Wearing long pants and long sleeves in warm weather
- Feelings of low self-esteem
- Difficulty handling feelings
- Trouble at school or at home

If you suspect a friend is self-injuring, talk to her without being accusatory. Tell her, "I've noticed you've had a lot of cuts on your arms lately, and I'm really concerned." Take time to listen and take her seriously. If she denies she has a problem, tell her how much she means to you and cite specific examples. For instance, say, "I noticed you have a new cut on your leg, but you tried to cover it up when I asked about it. I feel really worried." Ask her what she's feeling, then help her to find other ways of dealing with these feelings. Encourage her to go to her doctor or the school counselor. There *is* help for self-injurers. They just have to reach out.

If your friend asks you to keep her behavior a secret, you might feel conflicted. You want to respect her wishes, but you want to help her, too. If you think her life is in danger, you need to seek help as soon as possible—whether she wants you to or not. Even if she's mad at you afterward, tell a parent or teacher or call SAFE (Self Abuse Finally Ends) at 800-DON'T-CUT. You just might be saving her life.

Surviving Sexual Abuse

Unfortunately, statistics show that one in three women in America will be the victim of sexual assault. When a friend has been sexually assaulted, your response to the situation is an important factor in her recovery. You can ease her pain with understanding, encouragement, and support.

If a friend has been sexually assaulted, it can be difficult to know exactly what to say or do, especially if you've never been in her shoes. When one of my best friends told me she was sexually molested as a young child, I didn't know how to react. I wanted to say just the right thing, but I didn't know what that was. Words just didn't seem to be enough.

The most important thing you can do is listen and be there for your friend. Be patient. Never be judgmental or blame the victim for the assault. It was not her fault. Don't criticize how she responded to the assault. And perhaps the most important thing you can do is believe her. Encourage her to share her feelings, but don't press her for details. Let your friend know that professional help is available through national hotlines such as RAINN (800-656-HOPE). Suggest she talk to the school counselor or a therapist who's trained in sexual-assault recovery. If she has been raped or molested, encourage her to report what happened to the authorities, but never approach her assailant yourself.

Throughout her healing process, let your friend know she is loved. With your help, she *will* survive. Her long journey to recovery will be a lot less bumpy when you're there for her every step of the way.

QUIZ
How Good a Friend Are You
When the Chips Are Down?

1. Your friend just called you in tears. Her grandma died. What do you say?

   a) "Ohmigosh, I am so sorry. How are you feeling?"
   b) "I don't know what to say."
   c) "Well, she was really old, right?"

2. You've noticed your friend Jamie seems seriously depressed since her last breakup. She cries all the time, and she's even mentioned suicide. You

   a) tell someone like a teacher or parent immediately. Jamie needs help.

---

b) ask your school counselor what you should do about a friend who's depressed, being careful not to mention any names.

c) tell Jamie that her ex is so not worth killing herself over.

3. Your friend's parents just told her they're getting a divorce. She's crushed. You

a) drop everything and listen to her whenever she wants to talk.

b) drag her to the movies to get her mind off her problems.

c) avoid her, because you really don't know how to act around her.

4. Your friend Ron tells you he's gay. How do you react?

a) You try to be as supportive as you possibly can.

b) You feel a little weird around him at first, but you eventually get used to the idea.

c) You tell everyone you know the news.

5. You've noticed your friend Amber drinks herself into a drunken stupor every single weekend. Do you say something to her about it?

a) Yes. She needs to know you care.

b) Maybe. You'll keep an eye on her drinking for a few more weeks before you decide.

c) No. It's none of your business.

6. Your friend Elyse's weight has dropped drastically over the past few months, and you're worried she has an eating disorder. What do you do?

a) Ask her about it, then tell her you're really concerned.

b) Call an eating disorder hotline and ask what you should do.

c) Tell her she needs to eat more.

7. You just saw a documentary in health class about self-mutilation, and your friend Joni is displaying a lot of the warning signs it mentioned. You

a) ask her what's up with all the cuts on her arms.

b) tell her about the documentary and see how she reacts.

c) stay out of it.

8. Your best friend tells you that she was sexually abused when she was four years old. You

a) tell her how sorry you are, then ask her if she wants to talk about it.

b) suggest she discuss it with the school counselor.

c) quickly change the subject.

When the chips are down, what kind of friend are you? Count your As, Bs, and Cs to find out.

Mostly As: Super Supportive
Every girl deserves a friend like you when the chips are down. Not only do you always know what to say, you know what *not* to say, too. And even if a situation freaks you out, you always stand by your friend no matter what. You rule.

Mostly Bs: Somewhat Sympathetic
You always try to do the right thing when your friend is in trouble. Sure, your sometimes fall short—but you get an "A" for effort. Your friends are lucky to have you.

Mostly Cs: Completely Clueless
When people are going through a crisis, they need their friends to be there for them, not leave them high and dry. But that's exactly what you do a lot of the time. Sometimes being a good friend means standing by your pals in uncomfortable situations. Even if you don't know what to do, doing the wrong thing is better than doing nothing. Remember that.

11

Changing the World

You and your friends change one another's worlds every day for the better. But just think what kind of an impact you could make on the world around you if you put your mind to it! Whether you want to save the environment, curb teen pregnancy, or stop gun violence in schools, there's no end to what you and your friends can do when you give it your all. This chapter gives you the facts on volunteering in your community, starting school organizations, and making a difference. With a little effort, you'll make the world a better place!

Making an Impact

It's *your* world. So when you get upset about something like gun violence, racism, or domestic violence, don't just assume it's someone else's problem. Since you're a global resident, these issues *do* affect you. And you don't have the right to gripe about them unless you get off your butt and do something.

You and your friends have the power to make a big difference. Together, you can help save the ozone layer, mentor young children in need, or build houses for the homeless. You just have to take the first step. But sometimes that's easier said than done. I know the main thing that stopped me from volunteering in high school was that I simply didn't know how to get involved. Where did I need to go, and who did I need to talk to? I wasn't lazy, exactly—just a little confused. But instead of taking the initiative and making a few calls to find out where my talents would be best put to use, I just shrugged my shoulders and blew it off. Boy, do I regret that now. Not only would my would-be volunteer efforts have looked awesome on my college apps, I'm sure I would have felt much better about myself and my future if I had done something more to make an impact. Instead, I spent my teen years watching TV and listening to my stereo—both fun pursuits, I assure you, but they didn't help anyone else out or make me a better person.

After doing a little research, I now know that getting involved is way easier than I ever expected. I had always thought, "Why would they want *me*?" But organizations are dying to have people just like you and me pitch in and help perform a wide variety of tasks—from stuffing envelopes to organizing fundraisers. They'll find something for you to do, no matter what your age or skill level. Even if you only have an hour a week to give, that's fine. I've volunteered at soup kitchens and homeless shelters for a few hours at a time. Every effort, no matter how small, will advance the cause. You *can* make a difference.

First, decide what cause you want to fight for. Check out the following list to decide what you're passionate about:

AIDS/STDs	Homelessness
Animal Rights	Human Rights
Child Abuse	Illiteracy
Discrimination	Operation Enduring Freedom
Domestic Violence	Racism
Drinking and Driving	Rape/Sexual Abuse
Drugs and Alcohol	Smoking
Eating Disorders	Suicide
The Elderly	Teen Pregnancy
Environment	Women's Rights
Gun Violence	World Hunger
Handicap Rights	World Peace

Once you decide what cause you want to volunteer your time to, check out the following options. But this list doesn't include *everything* you can do . . . there's always way more that can be done. The sky's the limit!

1. Write About It

If you really want to get your point across, never underestimate the power of the written word. You and your pals can gather facts about your cause on the web, in the library, or by contacting national organizations. Then ask the editor of your school paper or hometown paper if you can write an article about the topic and how it impacts the community. Or write a letter to the editor about the subject. Your opinion could have a major impact!

2. Get Political

Some people think it's not *what* you know, it's *who* you know that counts. I don't think that's entirely true, but it never hurts to know people in high places. That's why it pays for you and your friends to establish a relationship with your local legislators. Write them letters and stop by their offices. Let them know you're concerned about your cause and want them to do something about it. Provide them with background statistics and real-life examples of how this problem affects your community, then talk about possible solutions. If you think a legislator would never want to talk to you, think again. It's their job to serve the community . . . and you're an important part of the community. If you speak up, it's their duty to listen.

3. Join Forces

Join a local, regional, or national organization devoted to your cause of choice, such as the Sierra Club, People for Ethical Treatment of Animals, or Greenpeace. These organizations often coordinate events such as walk-a-thons, food drives, and picket-line protests to raise awareness. Plus, they give you the chance to meet others who are passionate about the same things you are. Or you could start a pledge campaign where students promise to recycle, reject weapons, or practice safe sex—whatever your cause may be. If you want to encourage interaction among students and their parents, you can leave a space for parents to sign—for instance, the student pledges never to drive drunk and the parents pledge always to be available to give them a ride, day or night. Pledges such as these will help open up the lines of communication about topics that are often avoided or ignored.

4. Lend Counsel

Even though you don't have a Ph.D. in psychology, you can still help others in need by becoming a peer counselor, support group organizer, or hotline operator. Students often open up most easily to people their own age, so there's always a need for young volunteers. How do you make it happen? Talk to your school counselor about counseling opportunities in your school or check the blue pages of your telephone directory for hotlines and helplines (usually listed under "Community Services"). Call them for info on how to become a volunteer. Most hotlines offer free training classes monthly.

Another way to help is to start a mediation program or support group in your school to assist students in need. Ask your principal or school counselor how to get one started. For more info, see "Starting a Club" (page 189).

5. Get Other Organizations Involved

Once you find a cause you believe in, it's time to get others to join the fight. Say you're against drugs. You can ask your school clubs to join the cause by adopting an anti-drug theme. Ask the school paper to run stories on how this cause impacts students—like a feature on someone who lost her boyfriend to a drug overdose. Ask the art club to make posters illustrating the reality of drug abuse, then hang them around school. Ask sports teams to address ways to curb steroid abuse on campus. Have students wear red ribbons to spread your message in your school and community.

6. Bring People Together

Invite students, teachers, and administrators to join you for a forum discussing your cause. Once you discuss its effects within your school system and community, brainstorm some possible solutions. Interaction equals *action.*

7. Educate Others

Organize an assembly at your school and bring in a guest speaker to educate classmates about your cause. Or create a Web site or newsletter to get your point across, recruiting friends to write articles or submit illustrations.

8. Produce a Play

Produce a play at your school that educates other students about your cause and how they can help. You and your friends can write the script, design the sets, and star in the show. Lights, camera, action!

9. Raise Some Cash

Coordinate a snazzy fundraiser to raise bucks for your organization. Up the coolness factor by sponsoring a karaoke contest or an all-night dance-a-thon.

Changing the World

If something happens at your school that you don't agree with, you and your friends don't have to take it lying down. With a little patience, diplomacy, and enthusiasm, you *can* make a difference. First, figure out what your options are. If you're trying to change the "no shorts" rule at your school, find out if other schools have a different policy that is more to your liking—like shorts are okay, as long as they're not more than five inches above the knee. Then find out who has the authority to get the rule changed. Do you need to talk to the principal or the school board? Find out who has the power, then write a letter or make a call to that person, asking them what you need to do to get the rule changed.

Next, gather support. Circulate a petition at school for students who also want to see the rule changed. Remember, there is strength in numbers. Then get an attitude check. If you go in to the principal saying the no-shorts rule is "lame" and "totally old-fashioned," you're probably not going to get very far. Instead, think of the positive impact changing the rule would have. For instance, if the air conditioning in your school isn't so great, wearing shorts would probably make the sweltering weather much more bearable. And when students are comfortable, they're more attentive and less of a problem for teachers. Putting a positive spin like this on matters will make the powers-that-be more likely to listen to your argument than tune it out.

Finally, when you meet with the administration face-to-face, *look professional.* Skip the T-shirt and jeans and go with a skirt and sweater instead. They'll take you way more seriously if you look like you mean business.

Starting a Club

If there isn't a club at your school devoted to your cause, this doesn't mean you have to miss out. Just take the initiative and start one yourself! Starting a club will let you bond with your old friends while giving you the chance to make a few new ones.

If there's a national organization for your cause (like Greenpeace or Habitat for Humanity), contact them and ask how to start a campus chapter. Then approach the school's administration and get permission to start the club. More than likely, they'll have guidelines on establishing an organization—for instance, you might have to find a teacher to agree to advise the club before you can begin. Next, circulate a survey around school to find out how many students would be interested in joining. If it turns out that 400 kids want to join but you'd be more comfortable with 40, set a limit for the number of members. Then decide your club's main objective and design a format of the club's meetings. Make some posters announcing your first meeting and hang them around school. Buy some snacks and refreshments to feed your troops, and you're good to go. You've officially got yourself a club!

More Things You and Your Pals Can Do for the Community

Organize a food drive to feed your town's less fortunate

Adopt a family at the holidays

Volunteer at the hospital or hospice

Visit the local old folks' home

Serve food at a soup kitchen

Play with the puppies at the animal shelter

Tutor at a nearby elementary school

Make new kids at your school feel at home

Mentor a child in need

Greet new neighbors with a welcome basket

Do Something

There is a really cool organization called "Do Something" that helps match students with volunteer opportunities. It was founded by actor Andrew Shue of *Melrose Place* fame. You can find them at www.dosomething.org. I highly recommend checking it out!

A Final Thought

You and your pals have so much to offer. When you give a little of your time and effort back to the community, you are going to feel amazing about yourself and your friendships. Sure, your volunteer efforts will look beyond great on your college applications, and that's awesome. But what's even *more* awesome is the fact that they'll make you a better person and a better friend. So don't wait. Do it now!

QUIZ
What Kind of an Impact Do You and Your Friends Make?

1. Summer vacation starts in a week, and so far you and your pals have zero plans. You

    a) call around to see if you can volunteer anywhere.

    b) ask your friend if she has any bright ideas.

    c) resign yourself to three months of TV-watching.

2. For some strange reason, your school has decided to ban all future dances. You're so mad, you can't see straight! What's your next move?

    a) You circulate a petition around school, demanding that the dances be reinstated pronto.

    b) You write an anonymous letter to the principal.

    c) You tell everyone who'll listen that your school sucks.

3. A lot of kids at your school have been talking about huffing lately, and you're worried. But you're

certain that a school assembly about the dangers of huffing would really help. You

    a) organize one yourself.

    b) ask the health teacher to put one together.

    c) think about it some more but do nothing.

4. You're totally into animal rights. When your biology teacher announces the class will be dissecting frogs, you

    a) take a stand and refuse to cut up Kermit.

    b) ask the teacher if you can do a simulated dissection on the computer instead.

    c) close your eyes and do it anyway.

5. The school library just announced that it will have to discontinue its Teen Book Club program due to lack of funds. You

    a) get your friends together for a car wash to raise some cash.

    b) donate part of your allowance to the cause.

    c) say you're sorry to see it go.

6. They just installed a vending machine at school . . . finally! But you've noticed that people are throwing their aluminum cans all over campus. You

    a) start a recycling drive, then use the cash you earn from the cans to start an after-school environmental group.

b) ask the janitor to put another recyclable trash can by the machine.

c) vow to put *your* cans in the trash.

7. How many hours a week would you say you're completely, totally *bored,* with nothing to do?

a) less than 1

b) 1 to 5

c) 5 or more

8. Your best friend's grandma just moved into a convalescent home, and she tells you they're looking for volunteers on Friday nights. You

a) immediately sign up. It would be a fun thing for you and your best bud to do together.

b) visit the place before you decide. You need to check it out before you commit.

c) politely decline. You're not going to give up your Friday nights!

How much of an impact do you and your friends make? Count your As, Bs, and Cs, then read on . . .

Mostly As: Deep Impact
Congrats! You and your friends are definitely changing the world for the better. When you see something that makes you mad, you don't just gripe about it—you do something about it. Whether it's

organizing an assembly, starting a club, or changing a school policy, you're all over it. You go, girl!

Mostly Bs: Moderate Impact
You and your friends do make a difference. Maybe you don't do *everything* you possibly can to change a situation, but you don't sit on your butt and do nothing, either. If you just take a little more initiative, you'll be amazed at the things you can do. Go for it!

Mostly Cs: Zero Impact
Your motto is "That's not my problem." But if it affects you in any way, it *is* your problem. If something at your school or in your community is making you mad or needs to be changed, speak up. You and your friends have more power than you think. You just have to use it.

12

Friends Fallout

We all know what to do when a guy breaks up with us—call our pals, go through tons of Kleenex, eat lots of ice cream, and convince ourselves he's the Jerk of the World. But what are you supposed to do when a bud breaks up with you? As I know from experience, the loss of a friend can be just as devastating as the loss of a love—yet there are no books or articles out there on how to get over this sort of split. But that's where this chapter comes in. I'll tell you how to deal when a friend lets you down or dumps you, then let you know what steps to take if you're the one who wants to kick your compadre to the curb. Want to give your failed friendship another try? First, I'll help you know if you should even bother, then fill you in on my top-secret Reconciliation Recipe that works every time. Ready? Let the healing begin!

When a Friend Lets You Down

Every friendship is going to encounter its pitfalls now and then. But sometimes these pal-potholes seem too big for even the best of friends to hurdle. I'll never forget the time my best friend blew off my birthday party to be with her boyfriend. I was so hurt she would choose him over me on my own birthday. In fact, I was so disappointed, I wasn't sure we would *ever* work it out. Once we talked things over, however, we managed to patch our fractured friendship back together again. But it didn't happen overnight. When someone does you wrong, it can take weeks or even months for her to regain your trust. But it *can* happen—trust me.

What should you do when a friend lets you down? First, talk to her about it. Let her know how disappointed you feel. There will be no change or resolution without communication. You might be scared to rock the boat, but you'll do more damage by *not* saying something. Next, figure out if this bud blunder is something you can live with. If a friend told a mutual friend something you had divulged to her in confidence, that's probably something you can overcome. But if your pal slept with your boyfriend, obviously that's going to be a little harder (if not impossible) to get over. If you feel you can get over what happened, then give your friendship another shot. But if you feel you can't possibly forgive and forget, see "Ditching a Friend" (pages 200–203) for more details.

Once you've talked to your friend and decided this is something you can indeed overcome, it's time for her to redeem herself. She has to start at square one and earn your faith again. Let's say she blew you off, like my friend did on my birthday. From now on, she better be there when you make plans, come hell or high water. *No* excuse will be good enough for you. If she blows you off again, I'd subscribe to the "three strikes and you're out" rule. If she does it more than three times, she's outta there. You just don't need a friend you can't count on. Period.

But before you write any friend off, remember this: You're not perfect, either, so there are surely times

---

Disappointment Do's and Don'ts

DO: Talk to her about it.

DON'T: Talk to everyone else about it.

DO: Face the problem head on.

DON'T: Pretend it never happened.

DO: Try to work it out peacefully.

DON'T: Screw her over since she screwed you over.

DO: Realize that you're not perfect, either.

DON'T: Act like you don't have faults.

DO: Try to get past it once it's resolved.

DON'T: Bring it up every five seconds after it's over.

you've let her down, too. If you're tolerant and compassionate during the times she disappoints you, she'll probably be more understanding the next time you fall short of her expectations.

Bud Breakup

"I don't want to be friends with you anymore."

Those are nine of the harshest words in the English language. When my former friend Lavon told me she didn't want to be friends with me anymore, I was crushed. She had started hanging out with a new group of friends and told me I was just too "boring" for her now. I didn't know what to say. After all, she had been my friend for over three years, and she was the one I ate lunch with every day in the caf. Now, I felt totally isolated and alone. I remember spending many lunch hours in the girls' room because I couldn't face walking in to the cafeteria with no one to sit by. It was a really dark period in my life—but I managed to survive. And so will you.

If you've been dumped, you probably feel lower than low. Someone you've confided all your secrets to has thrown your friendship in the garbage. A major player in your life is now nowhere to be found. It can leave you feeling lost, lonely, and empty. You don't know what to do or where to turn.

First, call another friend for support. You need to

know that you aren't alone right now, and having pals around will help. Even though you're probably dying to sit around and badmouth the person who dumped you, don't. Instead, hit the mall, go rollerblading, or see a movie. The key here is convincing yourself that life can indeed be fun without your former friend.

Once the reality of the split sets in, you'll probably be feeling a whirlwind of emotions. Let yourself feel them all. Cry. Scream. Pout. Yell. Kick things. Don't censor yourself. Expressing your feelings is an important part of the healing process. Let yourself go.

Once a little time has passed, you might feel you want some more answers. Why did your friend choose to do this? Why does she never want to see you again? Wait at least a week so you have some perspective on the situation, then call her and see if you can meet for a talk. If you don't get the answers you need, it might be harder to move on. But don't be surprised if she tells you she won't meet you. When friends dump other friends, they often want a clean break. If she refuses to talk to you, you'll have to ask *yourself* what you've learned from the situation and leave it at that.

When you see her in the halls, how are you supposed to act? There is no right or wrong reaction here. After my friend dumped me, I pretended she didn't exist. That was the easiest way for me to handle the situation. But I've known ex-friends who are still quite polite to one another. You just have to do what comes natural to you. But hanging out with your other friends while she's around will let her know you've moved on.

And speaking of moving on . . . sometimes you've got to make yourself do that, even if you still love and miss your friend deep down. My friend Laura and I split about four years ago. I still care about her very much, but I've had to accept the fact that we'll never be friends again. Instead of sitting around wishing I were still friends with her, I eventually forced myself to get off my butt and made some new friends of my own. The lesson? Just because you lost one friend doesn't mean you'll never be friends with anyone again. All you can do is accept the fact that you weren't meant to be lifelong friends and then move on with your life. Who knows? The new buds you meet might be a zillion times sweeter than the old one who split. You'll never know until you take the leap of faith and open yourself up to new pal possibilities.

Ditching a Friend

Friendships are supposed to be fun. But sometimes the fun turns into frustration. Maybe your pal totally grates your nerves at all times. Or she's so negative, she's completely bringing you down. For whatever reason, you decide you want her out of your life—for good. But how do you know if you should definitely make the break?

How Mutual Are Mutual Friends?

When two pals call it quits, mutual friends often get caught in the crossfire. Here's how to survive in style if you're stuck in the middle:

- Don't take sides.

   Even if it's tempting, never gang up on one with the other if you want to maintain both friendships.

- Don't talk about one with the other.

   Your friends will probably want to talk about what's going on. But you can't talk about one without betraying the other one's confidence.

- Do things with them separately.

   Until things cool off, try to hang out with them separately. Bringing them together too soon will only set off fireworks.

- Give them a reality check.

   If they're acting totally weird around you now, say so. Otherwise, it will never work.

- Watch what you say.

   If you hung out with Jill on Saturday, don't tell Jackie all about it on Sunday. Some things are better left unsaid.

- Avoid surprise reunions.

   Sure, you'd like to see your friends make peace. But never invite them both over for an impromptu powwow. This isn't fair to either one of them, and they'll probably be mad at you for it.

Ask yourself "What does she really add to my life?" If she complicates your life more than she complements it, it's probably time to make a change. But if her good qualities outweigh her bad, maybe you just need to talk to her about making some changes to your relationship. Perhaps you need to see each other less or hang out in bigger groups rather than in one-on-one situations. Just be sure to really think about it before you do anything—because once you call it quits, it's never easy to rekindle a friendship and pick up where you left off. So be *certain* before you split.

If you decide your life would indeed be better without her, it's time to make the break. You can either do it in person, on the phone, or via e-mail. I think an in-person break is most effective, but you have to do whatever is best for you. Sometimes it's easier to express yourself in an e-mail or a note, but breaking up this way leaves a lot of things left unsaid. I once broke it off with my friend Jeff over the Internet, and we haven't talked in over four years. I'm sure we both have things we'd like to say, but the damage has already been done. It's too late. But it's not too late for you. Talk it out face-to-face, so you can both say what you have to say and have no regrets down the road.

Before you talk, make a list of the reasons you want to break off the friendship. Try to be diplomatic. If you want to break it off because she bores you to tears, try telling her, "We just have nothing in common." But if

Sure Signs You Should Split

1. You often dread seeing her.
2. You try to avoid her calls.
3. When you see her, you feel deflated instead of excited.
4. She frequently lies to you.
5. You don't trust her.
6. Her behavior puts you in danger.

there are major problems—like she takes drugs or lies constantly—tell her straight up. You'll be doing her a big favor by letting her know that her actions have negative consequences. If you think you could be friends if something changed, tell her what that something is. For instance, if she smokes like a chimney, say, "Listen, I just can't handle your smoking. But if you stop, I'd like to try the friendship again."

After your split, you'll probably run into your friend again—especially if you work together or go to the same school. How should you act when you see her? Be polite without misleading her into thinking you want to be buddy-buddy again. Smile, wave, and be on your way.

Second Chances

Friends break up and make up all the time, but it's not always easy. Sometimes, the pain and suffering you felt in your split just won't subside, souring any shot you have at a second chance. But if you can learn from your mistakes and use that knowledge to build a new-and-improved relationship, your story *can* have a happy ending.

Before you initiate a reunion, ask yourself: Do you *really* want her back in your life? Sometimes it's tempting to give people a second chance because you're missing close friendship, even if you're not necessarily missing *their* close friendship. Know the difference. And if there were major factors that played into your breakup (like drinking, drugs, or lying), have those factors been resolved? If they haven't, you won't have a very good chance at success the second time around, either.

Reconciliation Recipe

1 CUP OF FORGIVENESS: *You've got to forgive if you want a fresh start. No grudges!*

$1/2$ CUP OF HINDSIGHT: *What have you learned from your split that will help your renewed friendship?*

$3/4$ CUP OF OPTIMISM: *You've got to believe it's going to work out if you truly want it to.*

$2/3$ CUP OF APPRECIATION: *Appreciate the fact that friendship is fragile and precious. Protect it as much as you can from shattering again.*

If, after careful consideration, you *do* decide you want her back in your life, give it your best shot. This way, you won't have any regrets about the situation—and that's definitely a good thing. But make sure you have a long discussion beforehand about what went wrong the first time and how you can prevent those things from happening again. If at all possible, avoid playing the blame game. This isn't about pointing fingers or saying who was right and who was wrong. You're both after the same goal: a happily-ever-after friendship. If you work together, you can make it happen.

QUIZ
Can This Friendship Be Saved?

Before you decide to forgive or forget a friend, take this quiz to find out if your friendship can be saved.

1. Would your life be better without your friend?
2. If you broke it off with your friend, would you have no regrets?
3. Has your friend done something to you that you can't get over?
4. Do you dislike your friend?
5. Do you wish you'd never met your friend?
6. Does your friend's behavior put you in danger in any way?

7. Do you badmouth this friend with your other friends?

8. Have you ever dodged your friend's calls?

9. Has your friend ever lied to you?

10. Has your friend let you down more than once?

11. Have you blown your friend off more than once?

12. Has your friend blown you off more than once?

13. Do you and your friend fight more than three times a week?

14. Do you feel things will never improve with your friend?

15. When you talk to your friend about the problem, does she continue to ignore it?

16. Does your friend spread rumors about you?

17. Do you feel you can't trust your friend?

18. Do the other people in your life dislike your friend?

19. Is your friend controlling?

20. Will you feel relieved when your friend is out of your life?

If you answered yes to seven or more of these questions, it's time to write this friendship off for good. There are just too many problems. Friendship is supposed to bring you happiness, not heartache. Say good-bye.

13

Friends Forever

By now, you've probably got this friendship thing down pat. You know how to make interesting pals, resolve prickly conflict, and throw a slammin' party. You love the friends you have and you hope to keep them forever. But how do you make sure the pals you have now will be there at your college graduation ... and your future kid's college graduation? There are steps you can take *now* to make sure your friendship goes the distance *later.* Here is all you need to know about making your bond last. And last. And last ...

If you want to make sure your friendship has the staying power of the Energizer Bunny, adopt these top ten traits of together-forever friends:

1. Allow your friend to change and grow.

Your friend is going to change over the years (and so

are you). If you get mad at her for not being *exactly* like she is now, you'll lose her. Somewhere down the line, your best friend might get a nose ring or join the Peace Corps or start liking country music. She might vote for people you hate or do things you totally disagree with. But if you love the person she is deep down inside—her *true* self—none of that exterior stuff will matter. Your friendship will stand the test of time.

2. Accept the new people in your friend's life.

Your friend will meet lots of new people along life's journey. Some of these people will become really important to her. If you get jealous of every cool chick she meets, you'll have big problems. Just because she meets someone new doesn't mean that you've been replaced. You're irreplaceable.

3. Keep in touch.

Your friend might move to another state, another country, or another part of town. But wherever she goes, you have to make the effort to stay in touch. People's lives get busy, and many times they gradually drift apart without even knowing it. So pick up the phone. Write an e-mail. Send a card. Reach out before it's too late.

4. Let her make her own mistakes.

At some point, your friend will probably take a job you think is all wrong for her or hook up with a guy who is bad news. But sometimes you have to sit back and say nothing, even if you are sure you know best. When my friend Jenni was dating a guy I hated, I knew if I said something, our friendship would be finito. She was so in love with him, any negative word I said about the guy would have been like a stab wound to her heart. So I supported her through the relationship, never letting my true feelings be known. Once they broke up, I confessed I had never really liked him, and she thanked me for not saying something sooner. Even she admitted our friendship would have suffered—or ended—as a result.

5. Perform simple acts of kindness.

If your friend tells you she is having a big exam on Friday, ask her how it went on Saturday. If she bags on plans because she's sick with the flu, drop her off some chicken soup on your way out. Little things really do mean a lot in a friendship. You don't have to spend a lot of money to let your friend know she's cared about and cherished.

6. Be there in good times and in bad.

No one likes to deal with death or cancer or divorce. But when your friend is going through something like this, she needs you more than ever. When my mom was sick, many of my friends were nowhere to be found. They couldn't deal with it, so they simply denied it was going on. But the friends who did stand by me are the ones I'm closest to now.

7. Show up for the biggies.

Do everything in your power to be there (in person) when your friends graduate, get married, have a baby, or go through something equally important. These are once-in-a-lifetime milestones, and your presence will mean more than you can know.

8. Avoid loaning money to or going into business with a friend.

Whoever said you should never mix business with pleasure was probably right. Millions of friendships have been obliterated when pals threw business or bucks into the mix. You've been warned—so proceed with caution.

9. Be wary of living with friends.

A few of my best friendships broke up after we lived together. Even though it seems like rooming with a friend would be the perfect living situation, it introduces a lot of new factors into the relationship that are very stressful. You've got to deal with paying bills, cleaning up after each other, and being in each other's face—and space—24/7. It's not easy, and a lot of times it's not fun. Don't go there or proceed cautiously if you do!

10. Know when to agree to disagree.

If you and your friend clash on a subject, sometimes you've just got to accept the fact you'll never see eye to eye and move on. She's not going to change your mind, and you're not going to change hers, so leave it alone. Bringing it up over and over again will ensure that your friendship won't last five months, much less five years.

Going the Distance

It takes some work to make a friendship last a lifetime, but it's so worth it. Your oldest friends are often your best friends. They're the ones who've been there through it all—your first love, your first car, your first *everything*. They know you better than anyone else. And they're the ones who will be there for you anytime day or night, no questions asked. Who could ask for anything more?

QUIZ
What's Your Friends-Forever Potential?

1. Your best friend just started listening to rap, and you hate rap. You

   a) borrow a few of her CDs and give it a chance.
   b) tell her you're not into it, but it's cool that she is.
   c) tell her not to play it around you ever.

2. When your best friend tells you she met a new friend, what's your reaction?

    a) "Cool! I can't wait to meet her!"

    b) "Is she cooler than I am?"

    c) "Does this mean I've been replaced?"

3. You and your best friend have decided to go to different colleges. You

    a) e-mail and call her on a regular basis.

    b) see her during holiday breaks and summer vacations.

    c) eventually lose touch.

4. You think your friend is spending way too much time on the internet these days. You

    a) try to get her out of the house by asking her to the movies and the mall.

    b) ask her if she wants to talk about it.

    c) tell her she's becoming a total computer geek.

5. Last week, your pal sprained her ankle while playing golf. You

    a) bring her some homemade chocolate-chip cookies with a note that says, "FORE! You."

    b) send her a card.

    c) tell her to get well soon.

6. Your pal's eighteenth birthday party falls on the same night as your boss's annual barbeque blowout—a definite don't-miss event. You

    a) tell your boss you can't make it, then go to your friend's birthday party instead.

    b) go to your friend's birthday party first, and stop by your boss's barbeque later.

    c) tell your friend you've got other plans.

7. Your friend asks if she can borrow fifty bucks, but you're pretty sure she'll never pay you back. You

    a) tell her you don't like to lend money to friends.

    b) ask her to sign an IOU before you lend it to her.

    c) give her the money, even though you doubt you'll ever see it again.

8. Your friend is an avid meat-eater and you're a vegetarian. When you go out to a restaurant, you

    a) bite your tongue when she orders the porterhouse steak.

    b) suggest that she try the veggie burger, then drop the subject.

    c) get into a huge fight about animal rights before you even order.

What's your Friends-Forever Potential? Tally up your A, B, and Cs to find out.

Mostly As: Friends Forever
You and your pals have the staying power to be friends for life. All of the elements for an eternal bond are there: You let them grow and make their own mistakes. You stick by them in good times and in bad. And you're always doing little things to make them feel like they matter a lot. When it comes to friendship, you're true blue.

Mostly Bs: Friends for a Long Time
You and your friends share a special bond, and it's likely that you'll be close for a very long time. But will you still be buds fifty years from now? That's questionable. Sometimes you get freaked when your pals meet someone new or do something you don't agree with. But if you don't let your friends grow, your friendship won't grow, either. Just let your buds follow their own path, and you'll be pals for life.

Mostly Cs: Friends for Five Minutes
At this point, there's no way your friendship will go the distance unless some major changes are made. You've got to accept the fact that you can't change or control your pals. In fact, the only person you can change or control is *yourself.* So start by changing the way you treat your friends. Instead of judging them, support them. Rather than criticizing them, embrace them—flaws and all. That, my friend, is the true secret of a together-forever bond.

CONCLUSION

Now you've heard everything I know about friends. I truly hope what you've learned helps you in your own friendships. Remember: No friendship is perfect, but even a flawed friendship can make you perfectly happy if you love the person as deeply as I love my friends. The day I got married, I looked out into the audience and saw the people who mean the most to me. The history of my life isn't found in a textbook; it's found in the faces of my friends. When I looked at Sandy, I remembered the time junior year we got busted for staying out past curfew. One look at Jenni brought back the time she held me as I cried over the loss of my first love. And a glance at Stuart brought back all the highs and lows of college life. These people are my living history, and I wouldn't trade them for the world. Because they *are* my world. I wish that same level of friendship and commitment for you.

If you have any questions, feel free to e-mail them to me at FriendExpert@aol.com. I'll be psyched to hear how much your friendships deepen and grow.

Love, Julie

INDEX

abuse
   by boyfriends, 135–36
   sexual, 175–76, 178
acquaintance, best friend vs., 90
acronyms, note-writing, 124–25
activism, 181–94
adventurous activities, 49
advice seeking/giving, 23, 119
after-school jobs, friends and,
      41, 73, 81
age, friendship and, 74–76, 82
Al-Anon/Alateen, 170
alcohol abuse, 166–70, 177–78
anger. *See* fights/disagreements
anorexia warning signs, 171
answering machine messages,
      123
arguments. *See* fights/disagree-
      ments
authority figures, as friends,
      71–74

badmouthing, 57, 87, 199
best friend (Best Bud), 86–95
   acquaintance vs., 90
   being hurt by, 196–98

boyfriends and, 131–32, 143
characteristics of, 31–32, 35,
      86–88
finding, 85–86
lifelong, 207–14
long-distance, 77–78, 83, 208
new friendships and, 90–93
symbolic tokens for, 89
birthdays, 49, 147–49, 155, 156
boss, friendship with, 73, 81
Boy Bud (boy friend)
   boyfriends vs., 21–22, 67–68,
      81
   characteristics of, 21–22, 36,
      68
   coming out by, 165, 166, 177
boyfriends, 131–46
   abusive, 134, 135–36
   blowing off friends for, 56,
      132, 142
   Boy Buds vs., 21–22, 67–68,
      81
   breakups and, 139–41,
      144–45, 163
   double dates and, 136–37
   ex-girlfriend of, 79–80, 83

boyfriends (*cont.*)
  of friends', 132–36
  friends of, 78–79
  rules of good friendship and,
    56
  set ups and, 137, 144
breakup, friendship
  as initiator of, 200–203
  as object of, 198–200
  second chances, 203–5
breakup, romantic, 16, 26, 27
  dealing with, 34, 139–41,
    144–45, 163
bulimia warning signs, 172
business partners, 210

causes. *See* activism
chat rooms, 28, 82
The Clone, characteristics of,
    24–26, 36
clothing favorites, 35
  of Boy Bud, 21
  of Clone, 24
  of Cyber Pal, 28
  of Fashion Diva, 29–31
  of Gossip Queen, 26
  of Old Friend, 22
  of Party Pal, 16
  of Plastic Pal, 19
  of Study Buddy, 18
clothing trades, 48
clubs, starting, 189
coming out, gay/lesbian,
    164–66, 177
common interests, 42
communication, 115–29
  of anger, 99, 102, 114, 118,
    119–20
  consolation on breakup,
    139–41
  about failed friendship, 202
  about friend's betrayal, 96–98
  listening skills and, 57–59
  of support, 161

ten rules of, 116–20
  See also conversation; talk
    topics
community action, 190–91
competitiveness, 107–9
computers. *See* Cyber Pal; e-
    mail
conversation
  with boyfriend's parents, 78
  as favorite activity, 33, 36,
    64–65
  listening skills and, 57–59
  See also talk topics
copycat. *See* The Clone
crisis situations, 159–79, 209
Cyber Pal, 28–29, 37, 76–77,
    81–83
  cautions about, 29, 77

dads. *See* parents
dances, 41, 52
dangerous situations, 136, 203
  cyber cautions, 29, 77
  weapons possession, 106
dating, 136–37
deaths, 159, 160–62, 176
dependability, 40
depression, 161–63, 176–77
  signs of, 162
disagreements. *See* fights/dis-
    agreements
ditching friend, 200–204
divorce crisis, 163–64, 177
double dates, 136–37
drinking/drug problems,
    166–70, 177–78
  warning signs of, 167–68

eating disorders, 170–73, 178
  warning signs of, 171, 172
e-mail
  curbing angry, 104–5, 123
  Cyber Pal, 28–29, 37, 76–77,
    81–83

for long-distance friendship, 77

parental concern about, 123–24

as phone alternative, 122

envy, 107–9

failed friendships, 195–206

family, friendships within 69–71. *See also* parents

Fashion Diva, characteristics of, 29–31, 37

fights/disagreements, 97–114
  irreparable, 110, 195–206
  making up, 109–10
  no-nos, 98
  pitfalls for long-term friends, 210–11
  worst tactics, 99–106

fist fight, 106

flattery, 19, 20, 24, 25

food favorites
  of Best Bud, 31
  of Boy Bud, 21
  of Clone, 25
  of Cyper Pal, 28
  of Fashion Diva, 30
  of Gossip Queen, 26
  of Old Friend, 23
  of Party Pal, 16
  of Plastic Pal, 19
  of Study Buddy, 18

forgiving/forgetting, 105–6, 204

friendly gestures, 60–61

friends
  being there for, 40, 55–65, 86, 87, 141, 159, 160, 161, 209
  boyfriend dilemmas with, 131–46
  breaking with, 195–206
  communicating with, 115–29
  crisis situations and, 159–79
  doing for, 59–61
  falling out with, 195–206
  fighting with, 97–114
  importance of, 61–62
  keeping, 40, 55–65
  long-term, 207–14
  making, 39–54
  problem signs with, 203
  types of, 15–37
  unconventional, 67–84
  valuing, 55–57
  See also best friend; good friendships

"Friendship Coupon," 148–49

fun
  Boy Bud and, 22
  Party Pal and, 16–17
  Plastic Pal and, 20, 21
  ten fab ideas for, 47–50
  See also parties

ganging up, 102–3

gay friends, 164–66

gift ideas, 148–49

Girls' Night Out, 48, 132–33, 152, 153, 156

giveaway signs
  of Best Bud, 31
  of Boy Bud, 21
  of Clone, 24
  of Cyber Pal, 28
  of Fashion Diva, 30
  of Gossip Queen, 26
  of Old Friend, 23
  of Party Pal, 16
  of Plastic Pal, 19
  of Study Buddy, 18

good friendships, 55–65
  acts of, 60–61, 159–60
  anger and, 97–106
  boyfriend factor and, 131–45
  crisis situations and, 159–79
  envy and, 107–9
  importance of, 61–62
  as lasting, 207–14
  qualities of, 40, 55–59

good friendships (*cont.*)
  Ten Commandments of,
    56–57
  See also best friend
Gossip Queen, characteristics
  of, 26–27, 36
grandparents, 71, 155
gun possession, 106
guy perspective, 21–22, 68

hanging out, 33, 36, 41
honesty, 18–19, 20
  as friendship basis, 42
  salving feelings vs., 118
hugging, 109

ice cream, 109
indirect communication,
  103–4
insincere personality, 19–20
intellectual personality, 17–19
International Friendship Day,
  61
Internet. *See* Cyber Pal
irreparable fights, 110

jealousy, 107–9, 143
  best friend and, 90–92
"junk night," 48

knife possession, 106

lasting friendships, 207–14
  ingredients of, 40
lending money, 210
lesbian friends, 165–66
listening skills, 40, 56, 57–59
living with friends, 210
long-distance friendships, 28–29,
  37, 76–78, 83, 208
long-term friendships, 207–14
  Old Friend characteristics,
    22–24, 35
love, friendship and, 131–45

makeover party, 49–50
making friends, 39–54
  criteria for, 41–42
  meeting possibilities, 40–41,
    51
  mixing with best friend,
    90–92
  mixing with old friends,
    45–47
  pickup lines, 43–44
making impact, 181–94
making up, 109–10
mall, friends and, 41, 43, 51
manager, friendship with, 73,
  81
milestones, showing up for, 210
mixed signals, 103–4, 129
moms. *See* parents
mutual friends, 201

National Domestic Violence
  Hotline, 136
newcomers, as friends, 45, 53
new friends. *See* making friends
Nine Line, 163
nostalgia, 22–23
note writing, 124–25
"No way!" activity, 50

older people, friendships with,
  70–76
Old Friend, characteristics of,
  22–24, 35

pagers, 125
parents
  of boyfriend, 79
  death of, 159, 160–61
  divorce of, 163–64, 177
  e-mail curbs by, 123–24
  as friends, 69–70, 80–82
  phone call curbs by, 122, 123
Parents and Friends of Lesbians
  and Gays (FLAG), 166

parties, 16–17, 37, 147–58
    drinking/drug problems,
        166–70
    games, 151–52, 156
    hip themes, 149–50
    makeover, 49–50
    making new friend at, 44, 51
    slumber, 47
    special anniversaries, 153
Party Pal, characteristics of,
    16–17, 37
pen pals, 77
perfect pal, quiz to determine,
    33–37
phone calls, 120–23
    Best Bud topics, 32
    Clone topics, 25
    Cyber Pal topics, 28
    Fashion Diva topics, 30
    Gossip Queen topics, 27
    Old Friend topics, 23
    Party Pal topics, 16
    Plastic Pal topics, 20
phonies, 19–20, 23
pickup lines, 43–44
picnics, 47
Plastic Pal, characteristics of,
    19–21, 36
political action, 184

quizzes
    communication skills,
        126–29
    fighting style, 111–14
    friend-in-crisis, 176–79
    friend magnet, 50–54
    friendships worth saving,
        205–6
    keeping friends forever,
        211–14
    kind of friend you are, 62–65
    knowing best friend, 93–95
    love-friendship mix, 142–46
    making impact, 191–94

open mind about friendships,
    80–84
party-girl persona, 155–58
perfect pal, 33–37

RAINN hotline, 176
reconciliation recipe, 204
reliability, 42
road trips, 48–49
romance, friendship and, 131–45
rumors, 119

SAFE (Self Abuse Finally
    Ends), 175
sarcasm avoidance, 116–17
school
    adult friendships in, 72–74
    befriending newcomer in, 45,
        50–54
    making new friends in, 40–41,
        43, 44, 52
    note passing in, 124–25
    older crowd friendships,
        75–76
    organizing club in, 189
    Study Buddy, 17–19
school counselor, 73–74
screaming fights, 100–101, 114
secret keeping/sharing, 57, 79,
    88
self-injury, 173–75, 178
sexual abuse, 175–76, 178
shopping, 30, 31, 65
siblings, as friends, 70–71
silent treatment, 100, 101–2,
    113–14, 118
slumber parties, 47
speaking up. See communication
special anniversaries, 153
sports teams, 41
Study Buddy, characteristics of,
    17–19, 37
suicide threats, 163, 168, 176
superficiality, 20

supportiveness, 159–79
    best friend and, 87, 88–89
    Boy Bud and, 22
    loss and, 159, 160–62, 176
    Old Friend and, 23, 24
sympathy. *See* supportiveness

talk topics, 33, 36
    with Best Bud, 32
    with Boy Bud, 21
    with boyfriend's parents, 78
    with Clone, 25
    with Cyber Pal, 28
    with Fashion Diva, 30
    with Gossip Queen, 27
    with Old Friend, 23
    with Party Pal, 16
    with Plastic Pal, 20
    with Study Buddy, 18
    See also conversation
teachers, as friends, 72–73
Ten Commandments of Good
    Friendship, 56–57, 87
thoughtfulness, 43
    twenty friendly gestures,
        60–61
trading clothes, 48
trust, 32, 87, 88
    as friendship basis, 40, 42
    lack of, 203
truth-telling. *See* honesty
TV show favorites

of Best Bud, 31
of Boy Bud, 21
of Clone, 25
of Cyber Pal, 28
of Fashion Diva, 30
of Gossip Queen, 26
of Old Friend, 23
of Party Pal, 16
of Plastic Pal, 20
of Study Buddy, 18

unconventional friends, 67–84
    age differences and, 74–75,
        82
    authority figures as, 71–74
    family members as, 69–71

Valentine's Day, 138
volunteering, 182–94

Web sites, 28, 61
words to the wise
    about Best Buds, 32
    about Boy Buds, 22
    about Clones, 25
    about Cyber Pals, 29
    about Fashion Diva, 30–31
    about Gossip Queens, 27
    about Old Friends, 23–24
    about Party Pals, 17
    about Plastic Pals, 20
    about Study Buddies, 18–19

DON'T MISS JULIE TAYLOR'S
ESSENTIAL GUIDE TO GIRLS' *OTHER*
NUMBER ONE CONCERN . . .

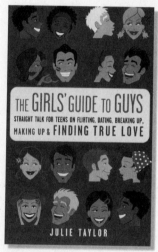

The Girls' Guide to Guys
0-609-80505-3
$11.00 paper (Canada: $17.00)

THREE RIVERS PRESS • NEW YORK